# ALBION R

# 2003

# A match-by-match look at
# Albion's 2002-03 season

*Glenn Willmore*

**Perspective
Publishing**

Also available from **PERSPECTIVE PUBLISHING**

| | |
|---|---|
| Albion Review 1999 | ISBN 0 9534626 1 7 |
| Albion Review 2000 | ISBN 0 9534626 2 5 |
| Albion Review 2001 | ISBN 0 9534626 3 3 |
| Albion Review 2002 | ISBN 0 9534626 4 1 |
| Albion Review 2003 | ISBN 0 9534626 7 6 |
| Bomber Brown: The Tony Brown Story | ISBN 0 9534626 0 9 |
| King of The Hawthorns: The Jeff Astle Story | ISBN 0 9534626 5 X |
| SuperBob! The Bob Taylor Story | ISBN 0 9534626 6 8 |

First published in Great Britain in 2003 by
**PERSPECTIVE PUBLISHING**
54 Newhall Street
West Bromwich
West Midlands B70 7DJ8

ISBN  0 9534626 7 6

Concept, book and cover design by Glenn Willmore

*Printed and bound in Great Britain by The Bath Press, Bath*

# FOREWORD

Albion's Season in the Sun was an unhappy one for their many supporters who had followed them through thick and thin for years in the Nationwide League. For the seven thousand season ticket holders that they gained this year, the experience of seeing Manchester United, Arsenal, Liverpool and the rest must have been a rewarding one, but for dyed-in-the-wool fans, it was a depressing campaign that had echoes of the traumatic '85-86 season. Many regulars felt betrayed by the Albion board's reluctance to spend during the January transfer window; just two or three loan signings — following the example of Bolton and Birmingham — would have been enough to claw back the season without breaking the bank. Certainly, the financial incentives, half a million pounds for each position in the table alone, seem to indicate that the effort, had it been made, would have been worthwhile.

Finally, the 2002-03 season, as well as being Albion's first in the Premiership, was also Bob Taylor's last at the club. Dogged by bad luck from the outset, he deserved better treatment for his ten years' service than he got — but the fans turned out in strength for his Testimonial game, to give him a great send-off. We wish him well in the future.

As usual, I would like to thank everybody who contributed to this book and towards *The Baggies* newspaper in the past twelve months, especially John Homer, Kevin Grice, Dave Holloway, Dave Hewitt, Colin Mackenzie and Robert Bradley.

**Glenn Willmore**
*July 10 2003*

*This book is dedicated to the memory of a true footballing gentleman, Alan Ashman 1928-2002*

*Attendance: 67,645*
*Referee: Steve Bennett (Kent)*
*Assistants: P Barston & J Devine*

# MANCHESTER U 1    ALBION 0

*Solskjaer 78*

| Roy CARROLL | 13-01 | Russell HOULT |
|---|---|---|
| Phil NEVILLE [71] | 03-02 | Igor BALIS |
| Laurent BLANC | 05-03 | Neil CLEMENT |
| John O'SHEA | 22-04 | Derek McINNES ❑ |
| Mikael SILVESTRE [76] | 27-05 | Darren MOORE |
| Nicky BUTT | 27-06 | Phil GILCHRIST |
| Juan Sebastian VERON [58] | 04-14 | Sean GREGAN [82] |
| Roy KEANE | 16-11 | Jason ROBERTS [69] |
| David BECKHAM | 07-09 | Daniel DICHIO [60] |
| Ryan GIGGS | 11-10 | Andy JOHNSON |
| Ruud van NISTELROY | 10-17 | Larus SIGURDSSON |
| Paul SCHOLES [71] | 18-16 | Lee MARSHALL [69] |
| Diego FORLAN [76] | 21-12 | Scott DOBIE [60] |
| Ole SOLSKJAER [80] | 20-15 | Bob TAYLOR [82] |
| Ben WILLIAMS | 30-07 | Ronnie WALLWORK |
| Paul TIERNEY | 39-21 | Brian JENSEN |

### THE MATCH IN BRIEF

The expected opening day thrashing at Old Trafford never
materialises, as Albion go close to grabbing a point — at least
until the harsh dismissal of Derek McInnes.

## THE BUILD-UP

*Monday: August 12:* Ipswich defender Hermann Hreidarsson spends most of the day at The Hawthorns negotiating a £3.2m move; but his £18,000-a week wages are a problem, and the deal falls through.

*Wednesday*: Andy Johnson hands in a transfer request, just three days before the start of the new season. "I believe it's to do with financial promises that Andy was made when he joined," says Megson.

*Thursday*: Albion sign Leicester's Lee Marshall for £700,000, and Megson seems set to get Millwall striker Richard Sadlier as well.

*Friday:* Albion go back to Tranmere to try to revive the Jason Koumas deal.

## THE GAME

After 114 years membership of the League (in its various reincarnations) on their Premiership debut, Albion set a new record in terms of the largest League gate that they had ever played in front of – 67,645 — which beat the previous record for the club of 67,440, set at Stamford Bridge on October 2 1954.

In for his Albion League debut, effectively taking the place of the unfortunate Adam Chambers, injured in training, was Sean Gregan, and he had a very comfortable outing in his first Premiership game.

United kicked off, and such was the quality of their passing that Albion failed to get a touch for the first couple of minutes, and but for a brave dive by Hoult at the feet of Veron, it could have been a disastrous start. From a Silvestre free kick, Giggs just failed to make a connection, and then, in the 11th minute, Roy Keane, the centre of attention in the game because of the impending £6m suit against him from Manchester City, had a shot saved by Hoult after a mis-header by Gilchrist.

Yet Albion could well have stunned the football world by taking the lead in the 28th minute — had anybody but Dichio been on the end of a perfect pull-back from Balis. Twelve yards out, the big striker, who looked lost in the top flight, barely made a connection as he swung at the ball. As a result, United were able to break, and they should have scored, when Keane, unmarked and in the clear at the far post, got confused between his boot and his head, and fluffed a header when he should have volleyed the ball home.

Hoult saved van Nistelrooy's diving header, but should have had no chance in the 34th minute, when Beckham played Butt in, who hoodwinked three defenders, including Hoult, but was unable to square the ball to the waiting van Nistelrooy, running the ball into the side netting.

Sixty seconds into the second half, United should really have had a penalty when Balis pushed van Nistelroy in the back, as he jumped for a Giggs cross, but the referee saw nothing. The ball was cleared to Roberts, via a United defender, and the striker took on one, two and then three defenders in another great run, but he seemed to lose his footing as he stumbled and shot weakly into the side netting.

Things started to get nasty in the 61st minute when Keane was booked for a nasty stamp on Gregan, when the referee should have played advantage on an Albion break. Mr Bennett then harshly booked McInnes for time-wasting on the free kick and then, in the 63rd minute, sent the midfielder off for a nasty-looking two-footed flying tackle on Butt; a straight red card. It was the earliest an Albion man has ever been sent off in a League season, beating Simon Garner's 1993 record (at Oakwell) by some 22 minutes.

Hoult was beaten in the 78th minute, when Butt slipped the ball through to – inevitably – **SOLSKJAER** – who placed the ball past Hoult for his 100th United goal

On came Bob Taylor, for the fading Gregan; earlier Lee Marshall had made his Albion debut as a substitute for Roberts, as Megson re-organised after the dismissal. Long-legged and ungainly, "Bambi on ice" as Leicester fans describe him, Marshall's first two touches were horrendous, and he did nothing useful thereafter, albeit in difficult circumstances.

United toyed with the ten man Baggies, and van Nistelroy and Solskjaer both missed relatively easy chances to add to the score.

*Attendance: 26,618*
*Referee: Steve Dunn (Bristol)*
*Assistants: P Sharp & M Cairns*

# ALBION 1                  LEEDS UTD. 3
*Marshall 90+1*           *Kewell 39, Bowyer 53, Viduka 71*

| | | |
|---|---|---|
| Russell HOULT | 01-13 | Paul ROBINSON |
| Igor BALIS | 02-18 | Danny MILLS |
| Neil CLEMENT | 03-06 | Jonathan WOODGATE[60] |
| Derek McINNES [73] | 04-21 | Dominic MATTEO |
| Darren MOORE [60] | 05-03 | Ian HARTE |
| Phil GILCHRIST | 06-12 | Nick BARMBY |
| Sean GREGAN | 14-10 | Harry KEWELL [82] |
| Jason ROBERTS | 11-11 | Lee BOWYER |
| Scott DOBIE | 12-19 | Eirik BAKKE |
| Andy JOHNSON [73] | 10-09 | Mark VIDUKA |
| Larus SIGURDSSON | 17-17 | Alan SMITH |
| Ronnie WALLWORK[73] | 07-05 | Lucas RADEBE [60] |
| Daniel DICHIO [60] | 09-07 | Robbie KEANE [82] |
| Lee MARSHALL [73] | 16-02 | Gary KELLY |
| Bob TAYLOR | 15-04 | Oliver DACOURT |
| Brian JENSEN | 21-01 | Nigel MARTYN |

**THE MATCH IN BRIEF**
In their first home game in the Premiership, Albion dominate a worried Leeds side, only to collapse and concede three goals to lose a game that they should have won comfortably.

### THE BUILD-UP

*Tuesday August 20:* The bid for Sadlier is brought to a premature halt when the Irish international is ruled out for most of the season with a hip injury. Megson turns his interest back to Lee Hughes.

*Wednesday:* Derek McInnes wins his first cap when he joins Scott Dobie on the field in Scotland's game with Denmark.

*Friday:* Albion claim to have agreed a deal with Coventry for Hughes... and Jason Koumas hands in a transfer request...

### THE GAME

Not lacking in confidence, Albion got off to a great start to their first home game in the Premiership — although not EVERY ticket had been sold — but even then you could see the difference between the two sides; Leeds always seemed to have more time on the ball, particularly up front. Early on Gregan had an opportunity, but his first touch was not great, and he ended up being rushed into a poor shot. Similarly, when set up by a clever Johnson pass, Dobie was too slow to make use of it. Then, in the fifth minute, Gregan was too slow in his own box, was dispossessed by Lee Bowyer, and ended up bringing him down from behind, for what could so easily have been a penalty.

Three times the ball dropped on the edge of the box for Derek McInnes, of all people, to take a swipe at it, each time the ball going high over the bar. But we should have scored in the 16th minute when Dobie went on a thrilling run that ended with Andy Johnson to sidefoot wide from ten yards.

It was all Albion, and by the end of the first 45 minutes they had created six decent half chances, but were incapable of taking any of them. In contrast, Leeds hit the post – an odd low shot from Danny Mills, which came out and rolled across goal – and created two other openings, one of which they converted.

The one they missed came in the 37th minute, when a beautiful back-heel by Kewell, to Barmby's pass, set up Bowyer, to lob wide with Hoult well out of position. They made up for that miss two min-utes later, when Mills went on a long run down the right, before crossing low. Moore stretched but missed, allowing **KEWELL** to sweep the ball home just inside the post. Just before the interval, Hoult could only watch as another Kewell shot whistled just wide, whilst at the other end Dobie had another opening, only for the Leeds keeper to make a brave dive at his feet.

Leeds were much better in the second half, having weathered the storm. Early on Harte clipped the bar from an in-swinging corner, with Hoult all at sea. They increased their lead in the 53rd, when another back-heel, this time from Smith, set up **BOWYER**, who clipped a beautiful shot over the stranded Hoult, and after that it was just a question of "How many?"

After Big Dave had limped off with a groin strain, the third goal arrived in the 71st minute, thanks to an error by Gilchrist. Attempting to boot away, he could only help the ball on to Bowyer, on the right, who quickly put over a low cross to the waiting **VIDUKA**, who had an age to bring the ball down, skip round Hoult, and roll the ball in. Had he not taken the cross, there were two other Leeds men in space who could easily have done the job. It was fast becoming a rout, and Albion fans were recalling Leeds' best ever win at The Hawthorns (4-1 in 1987-88, as it happens.)

With the ground now like a morgue, Marshall and Wallwork (his Albion debut, of course) came on for the last seventeen minutes. By this time another sub, Dichio was having an effect, and Albion perked up at last, and there were some exciting scrambles, two near things from Dichio, a near own goal from Alan Smith and a great saving tackle from Radebe, to stop Dobie.

Albion even scored their first Premiership goal, in injury time, when a couple of one-twos on the edge of the box led to the ball squirming through for **MARSHALL** to sidefoot home, at the Brummie Road End, on his home debut. How the crowd went crazy... Still, we always lose the first three games at the start of the season under Megson – don't we?

*Attendance: 37,920*
*Referee: Paul Durkin (Dorset)*
*Assistants: P Vosper & G Beale*

# ARSENAL 5     ALBION 2

*Cole 3, Lauren 21*     *Dobie 50, Roberts 88*
*Wiltord 24, 77, Aliadiere 90*

| | | |
|---|---|---|
| David SEAMAN | 01-01 | Russell HOULT |
| LAUREN | 12-02 | Igor BALIS |
| Ashley COLE | 03-03 | Neil CLEMENT |
| Martin KEOWN | 05-04 | Derek McINNES [61] |
| Sol CAMPBELL | 23-05 | Darren MOORE |
| Patrick VIERA [76] | 04-06 | Phil GILCHRIST |
| GILBERTO | 19-14 | Sean GREGAN |
| Sylvian WILTORD [81] | 11-11 | Jason ROBERTS |
| EDU | 17-12 | Scott DOBIE |
| Thierry HENRY | 14-10 | Andy JOHNSON |
| KANU [65] | 25-17 | Larus SIGURDSSON |
| Kolo TOURE [76] | 28-16 | Lee MARSHALL [61] |
| Jeremie ALIADIERE [81] | 30-09 | Daniel DICHIO |
| Ray PARLOUR [65] | 15-15 | Bob TAYLOR |
| Oleg LUZHNY | 22-07 | Ronnie WALLWORK |
| Stuart TAYLOR | 13-21 | Brian JENSEN |

**THE MATCH IN BRIEF**
Arsenal, with the pressure off, after their long run of successive wins was ended by West Ham, destroy Albion in a glorious first half display at Highbury.

## THE BUILD-UP

*Monday August 26:* Lee Hughes is given an ultimatum by Gary Megson, after stalling over wages — "Sign by Friday, or that's it!" Lee's wages, at £17,000 a week, are around £5,000 too much for the Albion.

## THE GAME

There was a ominous feeling in the back of most older supporters' minds as they walked past the myriad souvenir-sellers down Gillespie Road, outside the majestic Highbury stadium. The place was not the happiest of venues – quite apart from a fair few pastings we have received there, notably the 4-0 Malcolm McDonald hat-trick-inspired drubbing – there have been three FA Cup semi-final cock-ups, in 1937, 1978 and 1982, when we were favourites to win each time.

Arsene Wenger made two changes to his side that had grabbed a point at Upton Park on Saturday, as Bergkamp was injured, and replaced by Kanu, who was starting his first game of the season, and Ray Parlour was dropped in favour of Gilberto, with Wiltord being shuffled across the line. Megson was able to field an unchanged side, with Roberts and Dobie the front two looking for the club's first striker's goal in the big time.

Arsenal took just three minutes against the Baggies to mark the start of a destructive first half display from the Gunners. That's how long had elapsed when Kanu's long pass reached Cole on the left hand edge of the Albion area. In came Moore, but ended up on his backside and **COLE**  playing his 50th game for Arsenal — threw a shimmy before poking home a corker of a shot across Hoult into the far corner.

In the 21st minute full-back Lauren supplied Kanu on the right of the box, and he tricked his way through to cut the ball back for **LAUREN**, continuing his run, to fire high past Hoult with a clever shot on the turn.

Three minutes later, and it was three – going on eight – when Gilberto was gifted the ball in midfield (a regular occurrence all through the first half, unfortunately) and he gave the ball to Henry. Instantly he spread a long ball wide on the right, where **WILTORD**, in an offside position, ran in to stab the ball over the Albion keeper. Not only were Arsenal outplaying us, but they were getting the luck as well.

Things were much, much better in the second half. In the 50th minute Roberts booted the ball vertically up into the air in the general direction of goal; Cole made a complete hash of the clearance, and the ball ran for Scott **DOBIE** who, right in front of goal, just had to beat Seaman. He did – just – slipping the ball underneath the keeper for a lucky goal.

After that Albion were inspired, which only made one wonder what the evening would have been like had we been allowed to play that way in the first half.

Roberts set Balis free on the right, and he shot across goal when he really should have done better. Then McInnes won the ball and ran forward to test Seaman, and we were actually enjoying things at last – although that nearly changed in the 62nd minute when Kanu improvised a back-heel that was saved by Hoult with his legs, before being scrambled away.

There was controversy in the 68th minute when Keown hauled back Dobie as he ran clear on goal; referee Durkin allowed advantage to be played, and Seaman, given the extra time, saved well with his fingertips, but the referee should really have shown the former Villa man more than a simple yellow card.

The game was settled on 77 minutes when Cole murdered Sigurdsson for pace and crossed low for **WILTORD** to take the ball and skip round the defender to place the ball wide of Hoult. Two minutes from time Jason **ROBERTS** scored a good goal when he bustled his way past Keown on the right to fire home a low shot, but even the pleasure from that was negated in the last minute when **ALIADIERE** scored a sloppy fifth to send the Arsenal fans home happy, with their club sitting tidily on top of the Premiership.

*Attendance: 25,461*
*Referee:  Rob Styles (Hants)*
*Assistants: A Garratt & G Cain*

# ALBION 1   FULHAM 0
*Moore 48*

| | | |
|---|---|---|
| Russell HOULT | 01-01 | Edwin van der SAAR |
| Igor BALIS | 02-02 | Steve FINNAN |
| Neil CLEMENT | 03-03 | Rufus BREVETT |
| Ronnie WALLWORK | 07-34 | MELVILLE [60] |
| Darren MOORE | 05-11 | Junichi INAMOTO [60] |
| Phil GILCHRIST | 06-07 | Facundo SAVA [60] |
| Larus SIGURDSSON | 17-10 | Steve MARLET |
| Jason ROBERTS [88] | 11-17 | Luis BOA MORTE |
| Andy JOHNSON | 10-20 | Sylvian LEGWINSKI |
| Lee HUGHES [76] | 19-21 | Sean DAVIS |
| Lee MARSHALL [50] | 16-12 | Alain GOMA |
| Jason KOUMAS [50] | 18-09 | Zat KNIGHT [60] |
| Daniel DICHIO | 09-27 | Louis SAHA [60] |
| James CHAMBERS [88] | 22-22 | Steed MALBRANQUE [60] |
| Bob TAYLOR  [76] | 15-25 | Maik TAYLOR |
| Brian JENSEN | 21-26 | Barry HAYLES |

**THE MATCH IN BRIEF**

Fulham, unbeaten in ten games, are outplayed, in Albion's best
Premiership performance of the season. Darren Moore scores,
but SuperBob goes close to a wonder goal.

### THE BUILD-UP

*Thursday August 29:* Albion are linked with Manchester City's Shaun Goater, but Jason Koumas does put pen to paper at last, for £2m.

*Friday:* It's an expensive week, as Lee Hughes signs for £2.5m. Going the other way; Tony Butler, out on loan at Bristol City.

### THE GAME

After the frenetic (and frantic) enthusiasm of the Leeds match, things were on a slightly lower key for the visit of Fulham. For a start, they were incapable of selling their allocation of tickets; then again, so were we, and there were around two thousand seats unfilled when the game kicked off, compared with just 47 for the Leeds game.

There were other things that were different. Albion had three debutants; new signing, Jason Koumas, of course, whilst Lee Hughes made his second Albion debut – and, like the first, failed to mark it with a goal. Also on for his first Albion start, after coming on against Leeds, was Ronnie Wallwork. There was a League debutant on the Fulham side as well, with Inamoto attracting huge numbers of Japanese journalists into the press box after his stunning hat-trick that had won the Inter Toto Cup for Fulham, against Bologna in midweek.

That had earned the Londoners a UEFA Cup place, and meant that they were unbeaten in ten games, and were hot favourites to win the game. How wrong can you be, they were "out-possessed" 63-37%, and that summed up Albion's domination, which started right from the kick-off.

In the first minute Lee Marshall drove a lay-off from Hughes just over the bar from 25 yards. Ten minutes later, that was repaid when Marshall fed Balis who crossed for Hughes to fire in a shot on the turn from twelve yards that the Fulham keeper just managed to push wide, and Hughes should have done better when set up by Roberts soon after.

Then the game started to get silly, thanks to the ineptitude of the referee. He had a shocker, missing fouls, penalising minor incidents, and allowing the game to get away from him; he booked eight players in a game with hardly a bad foul, then missed a sending off for Brevett right at the end, for a foul on Taylor. He was awful!

Like the game against Leeds, Albion created a fair few chances, but missed them. Several times Roberts, whose touch was magical throughout, was within an ace of beating the last man, but never quite got his shooting boots on. Fulham had one half chance in the first half, when Hoult kicked out badly, to Boa Morte, who sent back a laughable shot.

Three minutes into the second half, and it was the Albion fans who were laughing, when the Baggies took the lead. It came following a series of three corners; at the far post Moore outjumped both Lee Hughes and a defender. When the ball came back to him, **MOORE** jumped again, and headed in off van der Saar's foot, for a scrappy but very important goal.

Soon after Marshall pulled his hamstring, letting in Koumas off the bench, but the Welsh international was fairly anonymous. Another Welsh star, Andy Johnson, should have added a second goal on 57 minutes when a fabulous run by Roberts ended with three men beaten and a perfect square ball for Johnson to put over the bar from eight yards.

Fulham had the ball in the net in the 62nd minute, but only with the aid of some pushing at a corner; that was the sum total of their threat. Albion, on the other hand, kept pushing right to the end, and the game will be remembered for something more than just being Albion's first Premiership win. What will go down in Albion folklore (and the distance out will grow with each passing year) was SuperBob's heroic shot from the halfway line in injury time. It was going in, until van der Saar caught on at the last minute and threw himself up to save. It would have been better than Beckham's...

*Attendance: 34,957*
*Referee: Andy D'Urso (Essex)*
*Assistants: SL Gagen & R Burton*

# WEST HAM U. 0    ALBION 1

*Roberts 30*

| | | |
|---|---|---|
| David JAMES | 01-01 | Russell HOULT |
| Tomas REPKA | 02-02 | Igor BALIS |
| Nigel WINTERBURN [83] | 03-03 | Neil CLEMENT |
| Michael CARRICK [73] | 06-07 | Ronnie WALLWORK |
| Trevor SINCLAIR | 08-05 | Darren MOORE |
| Paulo DI CANIO [73] | 10-06 | Phil GILCHRIST |
| Frederic KANOUTE | 14-14 | Sean GREGAN |
| Gary BREEN | 15-11 | Jason ROBERTS [83] |
| Edouard CISSE | 25-19 | Lee HUGHES [50] |
| Joe COLE | 26-10 | Andy JOHNSON |
| Sebastien SCHEMMEL | 30-18 | Jason KOUMAS [61] |
| Christian DAILLY [83] | 07-12 | Scott DOBIE [50] |
| Steve LOMAS [73] | 11-09 | Daniel DICHIO |
| Jermain DEFOE [73] | 09-17 | Larus SIGURDSSON[61] |
| Ian PEARCE | 19-22 | James CHAMBERS [83] |
| Raimond VAN DER GOUW | 17-21 | Brian JENSEN |

**THE MATCH IN BRIEF**
On the anniversary of the World Trade Centre Disaster, Albion record their first away win in the Premiership, thanks to a well-taken Roberts goal at Upton Park

## THE BUILD-UP

*Monday September 9:* Despite the luxury of a week off because of the international weekend, Albion are expected to be without Derek McInnes (suspended) and Lee Marshall (hamstring) for the trip to Upton Park.

*Tuesday:* In a bid to sell their allocation, Albion generously offer free travel for all ticket-holders at West Ham.

## THE GAME

Another minute's silence; twelve months earlier, we had attended the Swindon League Cup tie on the evening of the attack on the World Trade Centre. The atmosphere seemed other-worldly that day, and once again we all stood to attention to pay our respects, this time at Upton Park.

With Sigurdsson back from injury – but not Marshall – Megson gave a full debut in midfield to little Jason Koumas. Up front were Roberts and Hughes, but it emerged later that Hughesie was injured, and had missed training. It showed; he never got going, was not his usual self, and was withdrawn shortly after half time. West Ham – bottom of the table with just one point – started to swing the ball around. Most of the time young Joe Cole was at the centre of things, but their first chance was missed by the little midfielder, who swung and missed at Carrick's 12th minute cross, right in front of goal.

Sixty seconds later, Roberts skinned Repka on the right, and crossed low. Andy Johnson, running in, missed the ball, as did Clement at the far post, the move ending with a low shot from Koumas that James was comfortable with. It was a lucky escape for the home side.

Back came the Hammers, with Cole shooting wide, then having another effort blocked by Moore. Albion were relying more on attacking breakaways; one in particular, involving Roberts, Hughes and Andy Johnson came to naught when a goal really looked on. West Ham, were finding so much room on Albion's left, where Clement was constantly over-run – there was always a spare man there to pick up

the ball and sling it into the Albion box, as when Sebastien Schemmel put the ball over for Di Canio to scoop over the Albion goal in the 24th minute.

Two minutes later came the first real save of the match, when Hoult reacted superbly to push Cole's volley, from a Kanute cross, round the post. From the corner, the ball was once again fed to Cole, who forced another good save from the only England quality keeper on display that night.

On the half hour mark, Albion struck with the only goal of the game. It came out of nothing, Koumas spotting the opportunity to release **ROBERTS** on the halfway line with an instant pass. Jason beat two men, then streaked away to cheekily tuck the ball just inside the post, with James stranded in no-man's land. A quality finish, reminiscent of Cunningham at his best. It should have been two, two minutes later, when Roberts ran through on the left this time, but Balis carefully sidefooted his super cross into the side netting from 15 yards.

West Ham had two half chances before the break. First Cole wasted a free header in front of goal, then, right on the whistle Hoult just managed to beat Kanute to a long ball on the edge of the box.

It was Hoult versus Kanute again right from the restart, the Albion keeper doing well to save a stabbed shot with his legs at close range. It was the start of a torrid spell for the Albion defence, with a lot of home pressure, but, fortunately, no end product. Kanute shot wide, as did Cole soon after.

On the hour, it looked as if Roberts would score his second, when he displayed some neat skill in the box. James was fortunate to block his shot with his legs, and when the ball came out to Dobie, on for Hughes, he could not get his foot under the ball, and James caught his lobbed shot.

Gradually, Megson closed the game down, first replacing Koumas with Siggy, then, with seven minutes left, *Man of the Match* Jason Roberts with James Chambers. Albion leapt up ten places to ninth in the table.

*Attendance: 26,383*
*Referee: Clive Wilkes (Gloucester)*
*Assistants: T Massey & R Bone*

# ALBION 1    SOUTHAMPTON 0

*Gregan 80*

| Russell HOULT | 01-01 | Paul JONES |
|---|---|---|
| Igor BALIS | 02-02 | Jason DODD [83] |
| Neil CLEMENT | 03-03 | Wayne BRIDGES |
| Ronnie WALLWORK[HT] | 07-05 | Claus LUNDEKVAM |
| Darren MOORE | 05-06 | Paul WILLIAMS ☐ |
| Phil GILCHRIST | 06-33 | Paul TELFER |
| Sean GREGAN | 14-08 | Matt OAKLEY [70] |
| Jason ROBERTS | 11-18 | Rory DELAP |
| Andy JOHNSON | 10-04 | Chris MARSDEN [88] |
| Lee HUGHES [HT] | 19-17 | Marian PAHARS |
| Jason KOUMAS [63] | 18-09 | James BEATTIE |
| Scott DOBIE [HT] | 12-36 | Brett ORMEROD [83] |
| Daniel DICHIO [63] | 09-12 | Anders SVENSSON [70] |
| Larus SIGURDSSON [HT] | 17-20 | Tahar EL-KHALEJ [88] |
| James CHAMBERS | 22-29 | Fabrice FERNANDES |
| Brian JENSEN | 21-14 | Antti NIEMI |

## THE MATCH IN BRIEF

Gordon Strachan's lively Southampton side miss a whole host of chances, only for Sean Gregan to open his Albion account with a late fluke goal to send his team seventh in the table.

## THE BUILD-UP

*Thursday September 12:* Lee Hughes, who did not look at all well at Upton Park, looks likely to miss the Southampton game with a mystery virus. Scott Dobie, who came on for Hughes at West ham, is expected to deputise.

*Friday:* It looks as if Megson will have Jason Koumas (dead-leg) and Lee Marshall back in midfield, even if Lee Hughes misses the chance to play against the manager, Gordon Strachan, who took him to Coventry twelve months earlier.

## THE GAME

Megson gave his side an incentive for this game; if they won, they could have Tuesday and Wednesday off. If not, they would be in for training every day.

If it did work, it took a while to sink in. Albion were awful in the first half. With the midfield firing on one cylinder, and Hughesie still looking out of sorts with 'flu, it was clear that, with that formation, they would not score if we played all day. Southampton had a field day, and should have won the game well before we scored. In the tenth minute a great run by Pahars set up James Beattie for a shot, and it was just as well that Sean Gregan, playing in a defensive role in the first half, got in the way to block the shot. After that, every time Beattie came near Gregan, he got a good kicking...

Albion's first shot on target – just – came after a quarter of an hour, when Ronnie Wallwork's deflected effort trickled through to Jones. In the 18th minute, Marian Pahars made the first of his bad misses, when put clean through on the left by Rory Delap. With just Hoult to beat, he got his foot under the ball and put it past the far post.

There was a scare in the Albion area five minutes later, when Marsden floated over a cross from the left; Hoult went for the ball, but missed it completely; fortunately, so did Beattie. In the 44th minute, though, Albion generated their best move of the half. Roberts and Balis exchanged passes on the edge of the box, but the Slo-

vakian put a very acceptable chance over the bar from eight yards.

In first half injury time, the Saints went close again, because of a horrible mix-up in the Albion box which allowed Beattie to make a simple jump to head towards goal. The ball was bouncing gently towards the line, when Phil Gilchrist followed it in, to hook off the line at the last moment. Something needed to be done in the interval.

Megson's reaction was to bring on Siggy and Dobie, for Wallwork – who had an OK game – and Hughes. More importantly, he switched Man of the Match Gregan into midfield, and that made all the difference.

Even so, Southampton could still have won it even then, as Hoult made a key save from Pahars in the 59th minute, after Darren Moore had dived in recklessly. Six minutes later Moore brought down Pahars just inside the box, and was fortunate that substitute referee Clive Wilkes (in at the last minute for Eddie Wolstenholme) did not give the penalty.

Gradually – and Daniel Dichio played a significant part in this, along with the immaculate Gregan – Albion took over. In the 76th minute Gregan whipped in a sharp cross, and Dichio was not that far with a neat header. Even so, it didn't really look as if the game would be decided, until **GREGAN** tried a 25 yard pot-shot. It was a poor effort, for all of its dip and swerve, but Jones completely failed to handle the shot, which bounced out of his fingers and over the line.

Gordon Strachan's day was made complete five minutes from time when Paul Williams pulled back Roberts yet again, and, having already been booked for the same offence, got himself deservedly sent off. There was no chance of a way back for the visitors after that, although Hoult did have to save a late swerver from Telfer. Strachan was seething. "We had two good chances. They didn't even have one. Not even the goal was a chance. I had turned away, until I heard the cheers!"

*Attendance: 48,830*
*Referee: David Elleray (Harrow)*
*Assistants: D Bryan & P Norman*

# LIVERPOOL 2        ALBION 0
*Baros 55, Riise 90+1*

| Jerzy DUDEK | 01-01 | Russell HOULT ☐ |
| Jamie CARRAGHER | 02-02 | Igor BALIS [80] |
| John Arne RIISE | 03-03 | Neil CLEMENT |
| Stephane HENCHOZ | 06-14 | Sean GREGAN |
| Sami HYYPIA | 08-05 | Darren MOORE |
| Bruno CHEYROU [88] | 10-06 | Phil GILCHRIST |
| Dietmar HAMAAN | 14-17 | Larus SIGURDSSON |
| Steven GERRARD | 15-11 | Jason ROBERTS |
| Danny MURPHY | 25-12 | Scott DOBIE [35] |
| Michael OWEN | 26-10 | Andy JOHNSON |
| Milan BAROS [70] | 30-18 | Jason KOUMAS [HT] |
| EMILE HESKEY [70] | 07-12 | Lee MARSHALL |
| Salif DIAO [88] | 11-09 | Daniel DICHIO [HT] |
| Chris KIRKLAND | 09-07 | Ronnie WALLWORK |
| Djimi TRAORE | 19-22 | James CHAMBERS |
| El-Hadji DIOUF | 17-31 | Joe MURPHY [35] |

**THE MATCH IN BRIEF**
Once again, Albion look good against one of the top clubs, until they are hit by a sending off. Hoult is only the second Albion goalkeeper ever to be sent off; Murphy saves Owen's penalty with his first touch as an Albion player

*16*

### THE BUILD-UP

*Tuesday September 17:* With Albion facing four games in eight games, Megson hints that he might field a Reserve side for the Worthington Cup game at Wigan.

*Friday:* It seems that Scott Dobie will start the game at Anfield tomorrow, in place of the less than impressive Hughes.

### THE GAME

The Albion display in the first half was the best seen at Anfield since the early seventies. The defence was jittery, though. Liverpool tip-tapped the ball around, and had a few attempts at goal. Gerrard was in a good position, put under-hit his shot badly, allowing Hoult to tip it around the post. A few minutes later, Hoult made a marvellous save from Murphy's ten yard header that was going just inside the post, then reacted quickly to block Cheyrou's follow-up. The attacking play for that move had come down the Albion left, as so many did that afternoon – Neil Clement, who has not had a decent game for months, was at his worst, and should have been taken off at the break.

In the 23rd minute, Owen missed a good half chance, but then, five minutes later, it looked as if Albion had taken the lead. The ball dropped invitingly for Roberts, 25 yards out, and he smacked home the perfect half volley. It was soaring into the top right hand corner of the goal, when Jerzy Dudek leapt across, then, looking beaten, extended his leading arm to push the ball away. Good as it was, it was his only save of the game.

A game played in blistering late-summer sunshine exploded into life in the 35th minute when Moore made another serious error – and there have been a few so far this season for the popular defender. He let an innocuous long ball go, when it had no earthly chance of carrying to Hoult. In ran Michael Owen, and took it past Hoult with a great first touch, only for the keeper to wrestle him to the ground. No question about the penalty, nor the sending off.

On came Joe Murphy for a dramatic Albion debut, with Dobie being sacrificed. In the Kop, the whole of the Murphy family, all season ticket holders, couldn't believe their eyes. His first touch in an Albion shirt in the Premiership – and he saved an Owen penalty, diving low to his right to make a historic, if not particularly difficult save. Only twice before has an Albion keeper saved a penalty on his debut; Hucker against Leeds in 1987-88, and, just after the War, Norman Heath at Hillsborough. But to save a penalty with your first touch...

In the 42nd minute Roberts murdered Sami Hyypia with an electric turn of pace on the right, only to be brought down in the box. As Megson said, "They haven't given a penalty in front of the Kop for 45 years." It should have been a spot kick, and another red card, and Albion would have got something from the game. Elleray signalled that the Finn had got the ball first; we think not, as the replays confirmed,

Bizarrely, at the break Megson took off his best player, Koumas – who was brilliant at times – for Dichio, and the ten men sat back to soak up the pressure, possession going something like 88-12% to the Reds. In the 55th minute, Clement made a really shocking error, gifting the ball to Gerrard, who immediately whipped over a cross for new sensation **BAROS** to gently glide the ball, unmarked, past Murphy with his head. "One nil to the referee" came the chant from the sweltering, all-standing Anfield Road end.

It was all Liverpool after that, with Murphy showing great form in making two or three splendid saves, until Megson threw Moore up front for the last fifteen, where he caused a lot more trouble that the stumbling Dichio. The home defenders were really rattled, even though nothing much came out of it.

A minute into added time, Clement was once more humiliated by Murphy on the wing, he crossed for Owen to pull the ball down beautifully, and lay it into the path of John Arne **RIISE** to smash a perfect low shot in off the far post. Unlucky Albion.

Attendance: 25.170
Referee: Mark Halsey (Lancs)
Assistants: R Booth & P Dowd

# ALBION 0

# BLACKBURN R 2

*Yorke 71, pen, Duff 76*

| Russell HOULT | 01-01 | Brad FRIEDEL |
|---|---|---|
| Igor BALIS | 02-02 | Lucas NEILL |
| Neil CLEMENT | 03-03 | TUGAY |
| Larus SIGURDSSON [HT] | 17-07 | Garry FLITCROFT [19] |
| Darren MOORE | 05-08 | David DUNN [HT] |
| Phil GILCHRIST | 06-11 | Damien DUFF |
| Sean GREGAN | 14-20 | David THOMPSON |
| Jason ROBERTS | 11-21 | Martin TAYLOR |
| Andy JOHNSON | 10-22 | Egil OSTENSTAD [60] |
| Bob TAYLOR [64] | 15-26 | Henning BERG |
| Jason KOUMAS [HT] | 18-14 | Nils-Eric JOHANSSON |
| Scott DOBIE [64] | 12-09 | Andy COLE [19] |
| Lee MARSHALL [HT] | 16-19 | Dwight YORKE [60] |
| Ronnie WALLWORK [HT] | 07-18 | Keith GILLESPIE [HT] |
| James CHAMBERS | 22-04 | Andy TODD |
| Joe MURPHY | 31-13 | Alan KELLY |

## THE MATCH IN BRIEF

Bob Taylor comes in for his first start in the Premiership for the Albion, but the whole team fires blanks, before going down to a terrible penalty decision against Rovers.

## THE BUILD-UP

*Monday September 23:* Joe Murphy's penalty save, with his first touch in an Albion shirt, makes him only the third Albion goalkeeper to save a penalty on his debut, along with Norman Heath (1947) and Peter Hucker (1988).

*Tuesday:* The ball from the Albion-Preston FA Cup Final of 1888 fetches £32,000 at auction.

*Wednesday:* Derek McInnes signs a new two year contract.

*Thursday:* The Albion reserves go top of the Premiership Reserve League after winning 2-0 at Sheffield Wednesday.

## THE GAME

The rumours were true; Blackburn Rovers were indeed without their dreaded strike duo of Andy Cole and Dwight Yorke, and manager Souness was forced to play Egil Ostenstad, who had not scored a goal in the Premiership for four years. The bad news was that both former United men were on the bench, along with another in top winger Keith Gillespie. Could the Albion defence keep them out, whilst relying on a fragile attack to score the one goal that seems to be our lot these days – if we're lucky? No. But it took Rovers a while to get there, and when they did, it was down to a duff (not Duff) penalty.

The first half was tedious in the extreme; a form of cat and mouse. Rovers sat back and took the little Albion could throw at them, with SuperBob and Jason Roberts hardly setting the world on fire together. Albion's first attempt on goal came from Darren Moore, after a quarter of an hour; he powered a header just over the bar from ten yards out, after Balis had flighted over a tempting cross. He should have at least tested the keeper, though.

Four minutes later, Andy Cole roused himself off the bench, because of Flitcroft's head injury, and nearly set up a goal with his first touch, a clever back heel into the Albion six yard box. As the half went on, it was Rovers who came more and more into the game. In the 27th

minute Martin Taylor sent in a long cross into the Albion box, and when the ball was cleared, Damien Duff – who had a great game – fired a 25 yard volley just past the post. Not to be outdone, a few minutes later Tugay, who also had a great influence on the game in midfield, sent in another long range shot that had Hoult struggling to reach as it too, skipped past the post. In injury time, Duff got away from Balis and put over a great cross for Ostenstad, virtually unmarked in the middle, but the blonde striker mistimed his jump and, thankfully, put the ball over the bar. It was clear that there could be only one winner unless Megson switched things about a bit in the second half.

The manager's response was to bring on Wallwork and Marshall for Sigurdsson and, criminally, Koumas, who, for the second successive game, was his side's best player. The effect was minimal. Taylor had a shot blocked, and was thwarted by another last ditch saving tackle in the box, but with Roberts isolated up front – even after Dobie replaced Bob – there was never a chance of a goal if we had played all night.

At the other end, the Gillespie/Cole partnership that was already causing enough trouble, was enhanced by the addition of Dwight Yorke, and for long periods the Albion defence was under the cosh. It collapsed in the 71st minute, although in very unfair fashion, for when Ronnie Wallwork brought down Duff, the player was definitely outside the box, but fell into it. That was enough to fool the referee, who gave the penalty, and **YORKE** sent Hoult the wrong way, before making a point of going over the Albion fans in the Smethwick End to mock them.

Five minutes later the game was effectively concluded when Andy Cole's neat through ball sent **DUFF** away, the winger rounding Hoult to slide the ball into the net. For the last ten minutes Rovers had to play with ten men, as Yorke pulled his hamstring again, but it was little help to the Baggies.

*Attendance: 6,558*
*Referee: Lee Cable (Woking)*
*Assistants: P Nicholson & N Yates*

## WIGAN ATH. 3     ALBION 1

*Ellington 31, 61, 80*     *Hughes 89*

| | | |
|---|---|---|
| John FILAN | 01-31 | Joe MURPHY |
| Nicky EADEN | 19-22 | James CHAMBERS [HT] |
| Steve McMILLAN | 03-34 | Lloyd DYER |
| Jason DE VOS | 05-17 | Larus SIGURDSSON |
| Matt JACKSON | 04-07 | Ronnie WALLWORK |
| Gary TEALE | 20-25 | Des LYTTLE |
| Jason JARRETT | 18-16 | Lee MARSHALL |
| Tony DINNING [85] | 16-20 | JORDAO |
| Lee McCULLOCH | 10-18 | Jason KOUMAS |
| Neil ROBERTS [90] | 08-19 | Lee HUGHES |
| Nathan ELLINGTON [82] | 09-09 | Daniel DICHIO [62] |
| Mike FLYNN [85] | 12-12 | Scott DOBIE [62] |
| Lee ASHCROFT [82] | 15-03 | Neil CLEMENT [HT] |
| Leighton BAINES [90] | 26-28 | Matt TURNER |
| Ryan YEOMANS | 33-32 | Matt COLLINS |
| Paul MITCHELL | 02-21 | Brian JENSEN |

### THE MATCH IN BRIEF
Megson fields a grossly understrength side for an already difficult trip to Second Division leaders Wigan, and pays the penalty, as Albion are humbled in the Worthington Cup

## THE BUILD-UP

*Tuesday October 1:* "It's not just a case of giving the kids a chance. Some of the lads are tired and carrying knocks from Monday," says Megson, defending his decision to field a weak team in tomorrow's visit to Wigan.

## THE GAME

The arrogance of it all. Premiership "Giants" West Brom send a Reserve side to the JJB Stadium, and expect to dispose of a confident Second Division Wigan (who, incidentally, have the highest wage bill at that level). Except that it wasn't really a Reserve side – of those who played, only Lloyd Dyer was a true novice. The rest were players you would not be surprised to see playing in any game this season (with the obvious exceptions of Megson-rejects, like Jordao and Lyttle, both proven performers last season.)

Albion didn't lose this game because of the inexperience of youngster; they lost it because of a lack of motivation, and a total lack of interest from Megson. All the action for Albion fans came in the opening and closing moments. In the second minute Dichio was clattered on the edge of the box, and Koumas curled a free kick inches past the post, with Filan scurrying to try to reach the ball. Then, on a very slippery pitch, Wigan took over, and outfought and out played their illustrious visitors. Lee McCulloch shot into the sidenetting, Gary Teale shot wide, and Murphy – like Dyer, making his full Albion debut — saved well from Jarrett. After a quarter of an hour Koumas gave the ball away and it took some good harrying by Sigurdsson to stop Nathan Ellington scoring from close range. Just after, Ellington and Teale got in each other's way for a free header eight yards out — literally, Wigan were queuing up to score.

In the 23rd minute a really awful mixup between Sigurdsson and Lyttle – who will surely never play for the first team again – let in Neil Roberts who, eight yards out, lifted the ball over the bar.

Three minutes later, the same player headed wide, six yards out, after Teale had beaten the Albion's feeble offside trap. It was only a question now of when Wigan would open the scoring; which is when Albion had their best moment. It was another free kick, like the first one; this time Koumas' shot clipped the ball, and sent the keeper the wrong way before hitting the foot of the post and bouncing back into play.

On the half hour mark Murphy did very well to save a blistering shot from McMillan, but he was beaten sixty seconds later, when Matt Jackson headed back a corner from the left for Nathan **ELLINGTON** to rifle the ball home through a ruck of players.

In the 36th minute, there was a brief cheer for Jordao, who netted a Hughes knock-back, but the Angolan was offside. The second half started badly, and just fell away. The second goal, when it came, was a strange one, **ELLINGTON** looking offside when he collected Dinning's mishit shot, three yards out to the left of the post. He turned and fired past Murphy, with the Albion defence static.

An hour gone, and the potential was there for a real hammering. Albion couldn't put two passes together all night, unlike the home side, who went for goals. Murphy saved from Teale, Ellington missed a sitter, and ten minutes from the end, it was all over. Once again, **ELLINGTON** was the man in luck, completing his second successive hat-trick against a Premier side (he got three against Derby in the FA Cup) when he had a simple header, unmarked, two yards out, after Marshall had fallen over near the corner flag to allow Teale to cross perfectly.

For the last eight minutes Wigan brought on Lee Ashcroft, and had he not been so podgy, he would have scored a fourth, but his legs failed him at the end. A minute from time **HUGHES** hooked in a Lyttle cross.. A disgraceful performance, as Megson confirmed. "There were players out there who are paid to play in the Premiership — but it didn't look like it at times."

*Attendance: 52,142*
*Referee:  Chris Foy (Merseyside)*
*Assistants: P Norman & P Barston*

# NEWCASTLE U. 2   ALBION 1

*Shearer 43, 69*                    *Balis 27*

| Shay GIVEN | 01-31 | Joe MURPHY |
|---|---|---|
| Andy O'BRIEN | 05-02 | Igor BALIS |
| Kieran DYER | 08-03 | Neil CLEMENT |
| Nikos DABIZAS | 34-14 | Derek McINNES |
| Nol SOLANO [82] | 04-05 | Darren MOORE |
| Andy GRIFFIN | 12-06 | Phil GILCHRIST |
| Gary SPEED | 11-17 | Sean GREGAN |
| Craig BELLAMY [82] | 10-11 | Jason ROBERTS |
| Aaron HUGHES | 18-12 | Scott DOBIE [68] |
| Alan SHEARER | 09-10 | Andy JOHNSON |
| Laurent ROBERT [88] | 32-16 | Lee MARSHALL [76] |
| Jermaine JENAS [82] | 07-18 | Jason KOUMAS [76] |
| Lomana LUALUA [82] | 20-19 | Lee HUGHES [68] |
| Oliver BERNARD [88] | 35-07 | Ronnie WALLWORK |
| Shola AMEOBI | 23-22 | Larus SIGURDSSON |
| Steve HARPER | 13-21 | Brian JENSEN |

## THE MATCH IN BRIEF
The same old story; Albion play well, and take the lead at St.
James' Park, until a bad refereeing decision gifts Newcastle a goal,
and the home go on to win the game

### THE BUILD-UP

*Friday October 4:* Derek McInnes has shown no reaction to his minor knee operation, and may return to the side at St James'.

### THE GAME

There were eight changes from the Wigan game, but Joe Murphy kept his place because Hoult was suspended. Albion actually started off very well, and twice Roberts caused confusion in a slow United back four, on the second occasion running fully eighty yards before botching what should have been a simple pass to tee up Balis in the box. Then came a feverish spell of heavy attacking from the home side, but they made little impression.

In the 15th minute came the first poor refereeing decision, when Roberts chased through on a lovely Dobie pass, only to be dragged back by O'Brien, who should have been sent off, although had Roberts ran after the ball as fast as he subsequently ran after the referee, O'Brien would never have got near enough to him to pull him back.

Two minutes later Dobie showed a tremendous burst of pace down the left, ending with a shot which Shay Given did well to tip over. In the 27th minute. McInnes put over a free kick to Roberts, who held the ball up well before slipping it inside to **BALIS**. There the Slovakian got the run of the ball, off a couple of defenders, before cutting in to lash a shot into the net, through Given's fingers.

Newcastle were gifted an entrée back into the game in the 43rd minute. Over came a cross from the right, and Balis stuck out his right foot to clear. Six yards out, the ball went straight to Murphy, who picked it up. The referee decided that Balis had made such a suicidal pass deliberately, and gave a free kick on the edge of the six yard box, which Alan **SHEARER** lashed home through a wall of eleven Albion players. It was a shocking interpretation of the rules, that brought Newcastle back into a game that was clearly slipping away from them.

Predictably, there was more heavy home pressure at the start of the second period, with Bellamy missing a free header from five yards in the 48th minute – and the winger did the same again eight minutes later. In the 69th minute, Newcastle scored the winner, when a long free kick on the left was headed back across goal for the unmarked **SHEARER** to hammer the ball home. Nine minutes later, it looked as if Shearer had got his hat-trick – which would have been the second against Albion in four days – when he put away the rebound after Murphy had saved brilliantly from Bellamy, but the former England man was denied what would have also have been his 300th League and Cup goal by the linesman's flag.

Albion could still have saved it; in a late flurry, Given did well to save an acute shot from Hughes, and then, four minutes from time, Hughes and Roberts combined well for the latter to beat three men, take the ball right up to goal, then go wide, allowing Given the opportunity to save.

*Igor Balis, scoring his first goal of the season in the Premiership*

*Attendance: 27,021*
*Referee: Graham Poll (Herts)*
*Assistants: D Morrison & G Atlins*

## ALBION 1          BIRMINGHAM 1
*Roberts 87*          *Moore (og) 86*

| Russell HOULT | 01-18 | Nico VAESEN |
| Igor BALIS | 02-02 | Jeff KENNA |
| Neil CLEMENT | 03-04 | Steve VICKERS [90] |
| Ronnie WALLWORK | 07-26 | Oliver TEBILY ☐ |
| Darren MOORE | 05-24 | Darren CARTER |
| Phil GILCHRIST | 06-07 | Paul DEVLIN [66] |
| Sean GREGAN | 14-08 | Robbie SAVAGE |
| Jason ROBERTS | 11-25 | Darryl POWELL |
| Andy JOHNSON | 10-11 | Stan LAZARIDIS |
| Lee HUGHES [67] | 19-14 | Stern JOHN [84] |
| Lee MARSHALL | 16-19 | Clinton MORRISON |
| Scott DOBIE [67] | 12-28 | Curtis WOODHOUSE [84] |
| Larus SIGURDSSON | 17-10 | Bryan HUGHES [90] |
| Jason KOUMAS | 18-09 | Geoff HORSFIELD [66] |
| James CHAMBERS | 22-15 | Jovan KIROVSKI |
| Joe MURPHY | 31-01 | Ian BENNETT |

### THE MATCH IN BRIEF
Another sending off at The Hawthorns — but it does not pre-
vent ten man Blues grabbing the lead through an own goal.
Sixty seconds later Roberts hits a deserved equaliser

## THE BUILD-UP

*Saturday October 12:* No Premiership fixture because of international games. Albion appoint Tommy Moller-Nielsen as their European scout.

*Monday:* Gary Megson has compiled a 'video nasty' featuring all of the questionable refereeing decisions given against the club already this season. He intends to send the video to the referee chief Philip Don.

## THE GAME

For the first time this season, the gate at The Hawthorns cracked the 27,000 mark, for the first Derby game of the season, against Birmingham City.

Albion were up for the game from the start. Mind you, so were Blues, as Jason Roberts found to his cost. Three times in the opening few minutes Roberts was brutally hammered to the ground by Tebily, but referee Graham Poll decided that a free kick was punishment enough.

Albion dominated the first half, but what action there was, was pretty mediocre – "Like a Testimonial game," said Megson to Burrows midway through the half. Even so, Blues should have been ahead, against the run of play, for in the 26th minute Lazaridis skipped past three Albion defenders to put over the perfect teasing cross. John dived, six yards out, and had he directed it anywhere else, he would certainly have opened the scoring, but he sent it straight into the waiting arms of Hoult, who had positioned himself well to make a remarkable save.

The second half was much better, and started at a cracking pace. The first chance fell to Albion, when Marshall picked out Roberts, who raced clear, only to be thwarted by Nico Vaesen, who punched the ball away. Then Johnson shot just wide from 25 yards, before Vaesen made a stunning save when Marshall nipped in on a good Clement cross, to sidefoot on goal from close range. Then it was Lee Hughes' turn to race clear on the right, but he decided to shoot from an acute angle, rather than setting up Johnson, and the ball skipped past the far post. Finally, in an exciting spell for Albion, Vaesen saved well from Dobie – another one of Albion's 23 shots at goal (Blues had 11) all afternoon.

All hell broke loose in the last ten minutes. First Tebily was lucky to escape a second yellow card for pulling back Roberts yet again. Then Blues broke away down the left, and when the cross came over, Hoult was beaten by John's close range shot, but then he saved the follow-up from Horsfield and Clinton Morrison had a shot cleared off the line by Gregan in the ensuing scramble.

Eight minutes from time, Tebily tried it on once too often, pulling back Roberts as he raced onto a clearance, and, at last, Poll sent him off. In the 86th minute Hoult – shades of Seaman — lost track of Powell's left wing cross, and spilled it at the feet of Darren **MOORE**, whose instinctive reaction was to stab out a foot, which sent the ball into the net for an excruciating own goal.

Incredibly, a minute or so later, Clement released Roberts with a slide-rule pass down the left, the linesman gave the benefit of the doubt over Dobie being in an offside position on the other side of the field, and **ROBERTS** cut in, sidestepped a defender, and curled the equaliser just inside the post.

*Jason Roberts, late equaliser*

*Attendance: 40.893*
*Referee: Steve Dunn (Bristol)*
*Assistants: M Yerby & P Sharp*

# CHELSEA 2          ALBION 0

*Hasselbaink 30, Le Saux 52*

| | | |
|---|---|---|
| Carlo CUDICINI | 23-01 | Russell HOULT |
| Marcel DESAILLY | 06-02 | Igor BALIS |
| William GALLAS | 13-03 | Neil CLEMENT |
| Graham LE SAUX | 14-04 | Derek McINNES [57] |
| Frank LAMPARD | 08-05 | Darren MOORE |
| Mario MELCHIOT | 15-06 | Phil GILCHRIST |
| Quique DE LUCAS | 21-14 | Sean GREGAN [69] |
| Emmanuel PETIT [72] | 17-11 | Jason ROBERTS |
| Jesper GRONKJAER [78] | 30-12 | Scott DOBIE |
| Jimmy HASSELBAINK | 09-10 | Andy JOHNSON |
| Gianfranco ZOLA | 25-16 | Lee MARSHALL |
| Jody MORRIS [72] | 20-18 | Jason KOUMAS |
| John TERRY [78] | 26-19 | Lee HUGHES [57] |
| Oliveira FILIPE | 28-07 | Ronnie WALLWORK |
| Eidur GUDJOHNSEN | 22-17 | Larus SIGURDSSON[69] |
| Lenny PIDGELEY | 40-21 | Joe MURPHY |

**THE MATCH IN BRIEF**
Apart from a glorious seven minute spell midway through the
second half, Albion are comfortably tamed by resurgent
Chelsea at Stamford Bridge

## THE BUILD-UP

*Tuesday October 22*: The club's accounts reveal that the Albion made a profit last year of £2.6m, on a turnover of £14.3. Turnover is expected to double again this year.

*Wednesday*: Derek McInnes is out again, after a freak training ground accident when he landed on a training cone.

*Thursday*: Megson admits he is interested in Belgian defender Peter van der Heyden, currently with Bruges.

## THE GAME

Chelsea did not play very well at all, and it was easy to see how they had lost so disastrously to Viking in the UEFA Cup. Even so, they were usually too good for the Albion, mainly because of a lack of potent finishing up front, and a basic lack of ingenuity in midfield. The side that struggled to create a lot of chances in the First Division is really up against it now they are competing against better midfielders and defenders.

In the tenth minute at Stamford Bridge, Andy Johnson, Albion's most effective midfielder, put through a great pass that sent Dobie away, but Desailly did just enough to shoulder the Scot off the ball right in front of goal. Four minutes later Gregan supplied Johnson again and his tempting cross had Cudicini in trouble at the far post – but, of course, there was nobody far enough up to get on the end of it.

And that was Albion's threat gone for most of the game – until they were two down, at any rate. Chelsea stuttered, slowly, into life. In the 26th minute a great break out of defence from the home side saw Zola, the Premiership's top scorer, find Hasselbaink with a neat inside pass. The Dutchman actually rounded Hoult, but, under pressure from Moore, ran the ball out. He had more luck on the half hour mark, when Petit tried an optimistic through ball which fell for **HASSEL-BAINK**. This time he didn't attempt to round the keeper, instead clipping in a shot which hit Hoult on the leg, then slipped in off the inside of the near post.

There was little more to excite before the break, with neither side doing very much – but it was clear that Albion would have to move up a gear if they were going to get anything at all.

And all credit to Megson's side, they came out fighting in the second half, and dominated the early exchanges, only to concede a second goal in the 52nd minute. This time the creator was Hasselbaink, who turned Darren Moore inside out before firing in a left foot shot that was well cleared off the line by Gilchrist. Unfortunately, it came out right to the feet of **LE SAUX**, who had no problem slotting away his first goal of the season.

Megson threw on a third forward – which would have been a good idea from the start – and Albion had their seven minutes of near glory. On 63 minutes Clement put the ball in from the left, after a corner had been cleared, and Dobie rose to head firmly against the foot of the post, with Cudicini grateful to see the ball bounce back into his welcoming arms. Four minutes later, after Zola had missed a good chance, Clement smashed a brilliant 35 yard shot against the underside of the bar, and then, sixty seconds later, Cudicini made the save of the game, with his legs, from Lee Hughes. Not really worth the journey to the Smoke, nor the £30 admission (and the tatty £3 programme), not for seven minutes of entertainment, but it was nice to see a spark of his old form from Clement, back at his first club, and the faintest possibility that Hughes may recover his old scoring touch, sometime.

*McInnes — altercation with a traffic cone*

*Attendance: 27,044*
*Referee: David Elleray (Harrow)*
*Assistants: C Bassindale & P Norman*

# ALBION 1                    MANCHESTER C 2
*Clement 62*                    *Anelka 51, Goater 71*

| | | |
|---|---|---|
| Russell HOULT | 01-20 | Carlo NASH |
| Igor BALIS | 02-17 | Sun JIHAI |
| Neil CLEMENT | 03-03 | Niclas JENSEN |
| Derek McINNES | 04-24 | Steve HOWEY |
| Darren MOORE | 05-23 | Marc-Vivien FOE |
| Phil GILCHRIST | 06-19 | Danny TIATTO [86] |
| Sean GREGAN | 14-14 | Eyal BERKOVIC |
| Jason ROBERTS | 11-22 | Richard DUNNE |
| Andy JOHNSON | 10-05 | Sylvian DISTIN |
| Scott DOBIE [61] | 12-39 | Nicolas ANELKA |
| Adam CHAMBERS [67] | 23-10 | Shaun GOATER |
| Lee HUGHES [61] | 19-06 | Kevin HORLOCK [86] |
| Larus SIGURDSSON | 17-29 | Shaun WRIGHT-PHILLIPS |
| Jason KOUMAS [67] | 18-07 | Darren HUCKERBY |
| Ronnie WALLWORK | 07-08 | Ali BENARBIA |
| Joe MURPHY | 31-33 | Tim FLOWERS |

### THE MATCH IN BRIEF
Albion give their worst showing of the season so far against Kevin
Keegan's men; despite equalising through Clement's first goal of
the campaign, the defence falls to pieces

## THE BUILD-UP

*Tuesday October 29*: Former chairman Paul Thompson puts his 41,560 Albion shares — worth £2.9m — up for sale.

*Wednesday*: Midfielder Michael Appleton is given permission to go off on a mid-season family holiday, indicating that the club have given up hope of the player making it back into the team by Christmas.

*Friday*: As his former club QPR try to get him on loan, Daniel Dichio is banned to train with the youngsters after a bust-up with Megson that ends with him on the transfer list.

## THE GAME

This damp, dank day summed up Albion's season, and will be remembered by many fans as the day we realised our true level. City, who Albion beat 4-0 last year, could have had five goals on the break. The defence was horrendous, the midfield a joke, the attack, with no help for Roberts, virtually non-existent. Oh, Russell Hoult was OK.

SuperBob declared himself fit just before the kick-off, but did not even get a place on the bench, but there was a surprise recall, after a long spell out, for Adam Chambers, who had a pretty good game, it was his clever pass that set up Clement for a surprise snapshot that flew wide in the fourth minute.

The first half was poor, overall, with only four shots logged, and Albion having a slight edge, such that had it finished at the break, Albion would have edged it on points. In the 16th minute Andy Johnson sent in a shot which Carlo Nash took well enough at chest level.

In the 36th minute Anelka showed his first threat, cutting in from the right, but, fortunately, he failed to see how far Hoult had come off his line, and was eventually dispossessed by Moore. Six minutes later, McInnes sent Dobie away on the right, but his centre to Roberts was a poor one, and easily caught by the keeper.

In the opening minute of the second half, Roberts – who has won more free kicks than any other striker in the division – was fouled again just outside the box,

and Nash had some problems getting Clement's free kick away Five minutes later, Albion fashioned another promising attack down the right, but when Balis' centre was missed by at least two players of each side as it skidded off the wet turf, it fell for Clement, but the wing-back completely missed his kick and fell to ground.

City picked the ball up through Jihai Sun, who sent Berkovic away on the right, and he put over the perfect cross for the unmarked **ANELKA**, coming in late, to sidefoot into an empty net. Albion were behind for just eleven minutes. Roberts won another free kick outside the box, but it was advanced ten yards, inside the area, because of a petulant piece of encroachment by Berkovic, who was booked. **CLEMENT** smashed the free kick through the wall and underneath Nash, for his first League goal in almost exactly a year (in the last minute at Oakwell, in case you're wondering).

Albion never looked like winning it, though. Within a minute Hoult had to make a brave dive at the feet of Berkovic to prevent a carbon copy of the first goal. In the 71st minute Gregan, who was having a real shocker – and could well have been sent off for some of his assaults on Anelka – gifted the ball to City and this time when the low cross came over from the right, **GOATER** was there to stretch and poke the ball home.

Soon after Goater only just failed to get to a through ball would almost certainly have given him number three. In the 81st minute Gregan was trying to be too clever, by half, when he headed a high ball back towards his own goal. It went straight to Goater, who brought it down, but fired into the side-netting when he had two unmarked colleagues in the middle.

The worst miss came in the 89th minute, when Gregan was robbed by Anelka, who advanced and sent up Goater for a tap-in, but the Bermudian shot off the inside of the post, and across goal, where Anelka picked up and shot the rebound into the side-netting once more.

*Attendance: 23,638*
*Referee: Mike Riley (Leeds)*
*Assistants: M Cairns & N Miller*

## BOLTON W. 1          ALBION 1
*Dobie 16*                 *Frandsen 88*

| Jussi JAASKELAINEN | 22-01 | Russell HOULT |
| Bernard MENDY | 02-02 | Igor BALIS |
| Bruno NGOTTY ❏ | 05-03 | Neil CLEMENT |
| Per FRANDSEN | 08-04 | Derek McINNES |
| Jay-Jay OKOCHA | 10-05 | Darren MOORE |
| Ricardo GARDNER [82] | 11-17 | Larus SIGURDSSON |
| Youri DJORKAEFF | 13-14 | Sean GREGAN |
| Gareth FARRELLY [26] | 14-11 | Jason ROBERTS |
| Ivan CAMPO | 16-12 | Scott DOBIE [80] |
| Dean HOLDSWORTH [HT] | 18-10 | Andy JOHNSON |
| Anthony BARNESS | 24-23 | Adam CHAMBERS |
| Simon CHARLTON [82] | 25-18 | Jason KOUMAS [80] |
| Kevin NOLAN [26] | 15-19 | Lee HUGHES |
| Michael RICKETTS [HT] | 17-07 | Ronnie WALLWORK |
| Henrik PEDERSEN | 09-22 | James CHAMBERS |
| Kevin POOLE | 30-31 | Joe MURPHY |

### THE MATCH IN BRIEF
A disaster at the Reebok, as Albion — playing against ten men for
seventy minutes — decide to defend in depth, and lose two vital
points to a last minute goal from Frandsen

## THE BUILD-UP

*Monday November 4*: A surprise; Dichio is back in the squad for Saturday's game at Bolton. "We are all in this together; he gives us an option that we do not otherwise have," said Megson.

*Friday*: Now it's Jason Koumas' turn to get a tongue-lashing from Megson — "He should start playing like a £2m player." It's hard to shine when you are sitting on the substitute's bench...

## THE GAME

Having dropped into the bottom two by virtue of Howard Wilkinson's Sunderland's ability to battle for away points, Albion had a key game against their fellow strugglers, Bolton Wanderers, at the Reebok. The last visit there was a disaster – a 3-0 hammering in the second leg of the Play-off finals a couple of years ago. This one, they really could not afford to lose...

And, of course, Albion should have won it easily. They got off to a bright start. Dobie got on the end of a long crossfield Clement pass early on, but allowed himself to be dispossessed. In the eight minute, Bolton keeper Jussi Jaaskelainen got into a real mess with Ricardo Gardner, gifting the ball to Adam Chambers on the right hand side of the box, but his cross into an unguarded goalmouth was not good enough, and the ball was hacked away.

There could be little argument that Albion deserved their lead in the 16th minute. Jason Roberts had been fouled yet again by Ivan Campo, and from the free kick, 35 yards or so out, Neil Clement rocketed in a low shot, which fell for **DOBIE** to chest down and fire in a ferocious shot on the turn, to score a lovely goal.

Four minutes late came the incident which spoiled the tone of the game, when Bruno Ngotty appeared to elbow Roberts in the face. Immediately, referee Mike Riley – who had not long ago sent off two Bolton players in one game – showed the red card, and things started to get out of hand. After that, the home fans booed every decision, constantly

counted out every second that Hoult held onto the ball, and generally would up all the players. And it should have backfired on them, because Campo – already booked for fouling Roberts — should have been sent off as well, for fouling Jason again, dissent, and a tug in the box, but Riley, this time, bottled it.

What was worrying after that, until the interval, was that it was impossible to tell which side had the ten men, for the balance of play was about equal, although Albion should really have taken the lead two minutes before the break. Roberts went on a great fifty yard run into the box, setting himself up for a wonder goal, even though he got a tug from Campo – which should have been a second red card – as he shot, but the shot was high, and looped over the bar from just a few yards out.

The second half was all Bolton, as Albion camped back on their own 18 yard line, looking for a second goal only on the break. Almost immediately, Hoult saved a long shot from Frandsen only at the second attempt, then Okocha, who had a scintillating game, troubled Hoult on a couple of occasions. On the hour, Roberts carved out an opening, only for the home keeper to make a splendid block with his body, and that was Albion's last attacking contribution to the game; they just tried to shut up shop – and nearly made it. Mind you, had it not been a world class save by Hoult from Djorkaeff – three yards out – a couple of minutes later, we would have lost the game.

It was all Bolton – and how can ten men get 70 percent of the possession? And how is it that Albion, even with an extra man, look a poorer side than the bottom side in the division? Even so, it looked as if they had held out, until the 88th minute. Substitute Simon Charlton put over a routine cross from the left, nobody bothered to pick up Per **FRANDSEN**, and he picked his spot to power an unstoppable header past Hoult, from six yards. And had there been a few more minutes on the clock, Bolton would have won the game – of that there can be little doubt...

*Attendance: 27,091*
*Referee: Dermot Gallagher (Banbury)*
*Assistants: G Beale & R Burton*

# ALBION 0        ASTON VILLA 0

| | | |
|---|---|---|
| Russell HOULT | 01-01 | Peter ENCKELMAN |
| Igor BALIS | 02-02 | Mark DELANEY |
| Neil CLEMENT | 03-04 | Olof MELLBERG |
| Derek McINNES | 04-27 | Ronnie JOHNSEN [30] |
| Darren MOORE | 05-21 | Jlloyd SAMUEL [60] |
| Phil GILCHRIST [77] | 06-28 | Oyvind LEONHARDSEN |
| Sean GREGAN [71] | 14-12 | Thomas HITZLBERGER |
| Jason ROBERTS | 11-07 | Ian TAYLOR |
| Andy JOHNSON | 10-09 | Dion DUBLIN |
| Scott DOBIE [67] | 12-06 | Gareth BARRY |
| Larus SIGURDSSON | 17-14 | Marcus ALLBACK [60] |
| Lee HUGHES [67] | 19-11 | Steve STAUNTON [30] |
| Adam CHAMBERS [77] | 23-17 | Lee HENDRIE [60] |
| Daniel DICHIO [71] | 09-10 | Darius VASSELL [60] |
| Ronnie WALLWORK | 07-13 | Stefan POSTMA |
| Joe MURPHY | 31-08 | Juan Pablo ANGEL |

### THE MATCH IN BRIEF
No goals as Albion renewed one of the oldest Derby games in the world; Albion dominate the game, but it takes a great penalty save, by Hoult, from Dublin, to keep it goalless

## THE BUILD-UP

*Monday November 11*: A Burton inquest reveals that Albion legend Jeff Astle died from "repeated trauma from heading a football."

## THE GAME

This was a real blood-and-thunder game, with players committed to some very tough challenges from the start. The result was a thriller, the most exciting game of the season, and easily Albion's best performance in the Premiership. What a shame they could not get the breakthrough that might well have won them the game early on.

In the fifth minute Igor Balis pulled the ball back for Johnson – who got better and better as the game went on – to rattle in a shot that Enckelman spilled, Jason Roberts following up to test the Villa keeper again. Two minutes later, and Albion really should have been ahead, with the Goal of The Season tucked into their back pockets. After a little bit of Villa pressure, which had ended with an inaccurate snapshot from Gareth Barry, Jason Roberts broke downfield, running with the ball from well inside his own half. On and on he went, jinking this way and that, mesmerising two defenders — Delaney so much so that he ended up on his backside – only to lift his head at the crucial moment, and put the ball over the bar.

By the 20th minute Villa's short spell on top was over, and it was Albion's game again, with Moore trying an ambitious first time chip, and Enckelman saving again from Roberts on the near post. Roberts, in fact, had a great first half, harrying the Villa defenders, but faded in the second period, when it was Andy Johnson's turn to shine, although he first really started to sparkle at the end of the first half, when he severely tested the Villa keeper with a fine low shot.

Yet, as so often in the past, it could have been Villa going in ahead, for right on the whistle Delaney went through on the right, and appeared to be brought down by Gregan. Referee Dermott Gallagher thought it was a dive – but was not so sure that he wanted to book Delaney, and quite a scuffle developed between the players. The Villa men seemed certain that there was a foul, and they had a point.

There was little respite for the Villa at the start of the second half. Balis had a hard shot tipped round at the near post; Scott Dobie brilliantly cut in from the right, only to lose possession at the last minute, and Johnson himself managed to get in a couple of shots, sadly, as so often this season, well over the bar. Funniest of all was the mix-up between Ian Taylor and Allback, whose involuntary back-header almost went down as the funniest own goal for years, had not Enckelman performed miracles to palm it out.

Desperate for a goal, Megson threw caution to the winds, and brought on Hughes and Dichio to play three attackers. Not long after, it seemed that disaster had struck, when Barry went on a scintillating run on the left, beating three men before being tripped – according to Mr Gallagher, who was probably making up for his error with the first penalty call – by Darren Moore, who was booked. Dublin took the penalty, and certainly hit it firmly enough, sending Hoult the wrong way, but the Albion hero still managed to kick the fall away as he fell, to at least retain a point for his side.

There should have been a red card, as twice in a couple of minutes Barry manhandled Roberts to the floor in full flight. He was booked for the first offence, but the second was actually worse...

*Great penalty save from Hoult*

*Attendance: 40,113*
*Referee: Jeff Winter (Stockton-on-Tees)*
*Assistants: M L Short & R Martin*

# EVERTON 1     ALBION 0

*Radzinski 35*

| | | |
|---|---|---|
| Richard WRIGHT | 01-01 | Russell HOULT |
| Tony HIBBERT | 28-02 | Igor BALIS [72] |
| Joseph YOBO | 20-03 | Neil CLEMENT |
| Alan STUBBS | 04-04 | Derek McINNES |
| David UNSWORTH | 06-05 | Darren MOORE |
| Lee CARSLEY | 26-17 | Larus SIGURDSSON |
| LI TIE | 12-14 | Sean GREGAN |
| Thomas GRAVESEN | 16-11 | Jason ROBERTS |
| Gary NAYSMITH [84] | 15-12 | Scott DOBIE [51] |
| Kevin CAMPBELL | 09-10 | Andy JOHNSON |
| Tomasz RADZINSKI [88] | 08-07 | Ronnie WALLWORK |
| Wayne ROONEY [88] | 18-18 | Jason KOUMAS [72] |
| Alessandro PISTONE [84] | 03-19 | Lee HUGHES [51] |
| Steve WATSON | 02-09 | Daniel DICHIO |
| David WEIR | 05-22 | James CHAMBERS |
| Steve SIMONSEN | 13-31 | Joe MURPHY |

### THE MATCH IN BRIEF
It's a hard task for Albion, to take on the Premiership's form team,
Everton — Wayne Rooney and all — at Goodison Park. Albion
play well, but lack any punch up front

## THE BUILD-UP

*Wednesday November 20*: Both Scott Dobie and Derek McInnes win further caps in Scotland's farcical 2-0 defeat in the rain in Portugal.

*Thursday*: Gary Megson is not too pleased after he comes in for criticism at the club's otherwise routine AGM.

## THE GAME

Everton were the form team of the division, with five straight wins, and without having conceded a goal for over seven and a half hours. Well organised, excellent team spirit and a solid defence, without much individual brilliance. That was Everton this year – and Albion last season. This was also a gala occasion, in that it was one of the games used by the home club to celebrate their being the first club to clock up one hundred seasons in the top flight (as compared with Albion's 71 or so) and there were so nice touches before the game, and at half time.

Albion had the first shot of the game; a Scot Dobie effort comfortably fielded by Wright; six minutes later Naysmith had a fiercer effort which went straight at Hoult. We were lucky shortly after that, when, from a corner, Alan Stubbs had a header which was going in, only for his own man — Campbell — to stop the ball almost on our goal line.

Roberts was his usual frustrating self, with some nice footwork that ended with a shot just over the bar – just moments after being ticked off by the referee for moaning. At least he was threatening – the problem with the rest of the team was that, although they were solid enough, the forwards were never going to score if they played all day, and the midfield, lacking Gregan, in defence for the injured Gilchrist, could create nothing at this level.

The only goal of the game – and once it went in, you knew it was all over – came in the 35th minute. It was down to a sloppy clearance by Sigurdsson, and when the ball was put back to Li Tie, he slotted the ball into the right hand side of the box. In ran Canadian **RADZINSKI**, and thrashed a great first time shot between Hoult and the near post – although the shot was so good you couldn't blame the keeper at all.

Six minutes into the second half, Megson decided it was time to bring off Dobie and give Hughes a run out. He really, really shouldn't have bothered. Whatever it is that has caused a total lack of form with Hughes – and it's not just because he's not Premiership standard, because he barely looks Sunday League standard – it's still there. He was absolutely dreadful...

His striking partner, Roberts, should have shocked the home fans sixty seconds later. Some good work by Andy Johnson (who started well, but faded) led to a neat pass on the edge of the box, and Jason was in, but he was pressurised by Wright, and shot wide from twelve yards, claiming a penalty as well. It was a chance that should have been taken.

There was a narrow squeak when Gregan cleared a Gravesen cross off the line. Then a typical over-confident piece of defensive work by Gregan let in Carsley, who set up Campbell with a great chance, twelve yards out, only for the former Arsenal man to fall over. If that was bad from Gregan, four minutes later we had some high comedy when he tried to score a classic own goal. When Hoult saved the first effort, brilliantly, Gregan had another go, but miskicked twice more.

In the 75th minute Gregan was there again, ball-watching against Radzinski, who forced Hoult to another good save. In the 82nd minute Clement had the last Albion chance at the far post, but his shot was blocked. The match was completed by a cameo appearance from new star, Wayne Rooney, who looked as if he had stitched up Gregan like a kipper, to win a penalty, but the referee did not give it, then, hands on hip, he made Darren Moore look like an idiot. A precocious talent, indeed.

Fascinating postscript. There are not many times in their history when Albion have lost, but gone UP in the table, but because of West Ham's 4-1 defeat, Albion moved off the bottom of the table. At that rate, we'll be safe by Christmas...

*Attendance: 27,029*
*Referee: Paul Durkin (Dorset)*
*Assistants: M Yerby & T Green*

# ALBION 1     MIDDLESBROUGH 0
Dichio 73

| | | |
|---|---|---|
| Russell HOULT | 01-01 | Mark SCHWARZER |
| Igor BALIS | 02-15 | Tony VIDMAR |
| Neil CLEMENT | 03-30 | Stuart PARNABY [61] |
| Derek McINNES | 04-04 | Ugo EHIOGU |
| Darren MOORE [85] | 05-06 | Gareth SOUTHGATE |
| Sean GREGAN | 14-12 | Jonathan GREENING |
| Jason KOUMAS | 18-14 | GEREMI |
| Jason ROBERTS [89] | 11-07 | George BOATENG |
| Andy JOHNSON | 10-16 | Joseph-Desire JOB |
| Lee HUGHES [59] | 19-11 | Alen BOKSIC [76] |
| Larus SIGURDSSON | 17-09 | Massimo MACCARONE [74] |
| Scott DOBIE [89] | 12-28 | Colin COOPER [61] |
| James CHAMBERS [85] | 22-08 | Szilard NEMETH [76] |
| Daniel DICHIO [59] | 09-26 | Noel WHELAN [74] |
| Ronnie WALLWORK | 07-35 | Bradley JONES |
| Joe MURPHY | 31-31 | Luke WILKSHIRE |

**THE MATCH IN BRIEF**
Despite criticism from his team mates, Hughes gets a recall, but it's transfer-listed Daniel Dichio who chalks up his first goal of the season to beat unadventurous Middlesbrough.

## THE BUILD-UP

*Monday November 25*: It is leaked that Lee Hughes came in for some heavy criticism from his own team mates for his dreadful performance at Everton on Saturday."We might as well have been playing with ten men," said one unnamed player.

*Thursday*: Gary Megson is presented with the Lordship of the Manor of West Bromwich. Stoke manager Tony Pulis is desperate to sign both Dichio and Jensen on loan.

## THE GAME

For the third match in succession, the gates were closed at The Hawthorns, with the sell-out board going up for the visit of high-riding sixth-placed Middlesbrough

Megson made two changes to try and stop the rot which had seen his side go ten games without a win, bringing in Koumas and (surprisingly) Hughes – who had been criticised by his colleagues for his performance at Everton – for Wallwork and Dobie.

The game started scrappily, with players of both sides falling all over the place on a fast pitch made slippery by the heavy rain that began to fall shortly before the kick-out. Ex-Baggie Ugo Ehiogu, in particular, looked uncomfortable. There was no question which side was keener to win. Middlesborough were the most negative side seen at The Hawthorns for some time, and Albion, who put a huge amount of effort in throughout, dominated almost all the game.

Early on Hughes had a rather optimistic shot from wide on the right saved by Schwarzer, then Neil Clement sent a stupendous half volley inches past the post, with the Boro keeper a mere spectator. Twice more Clement went close to a goal, both times after being picked out by good passes from Koumas, who was having his best game since being taken off at Anfield. It was one-way traffic, but without the certainty of a goal – this Albion side is still far too lightweight in attack to guarantee at least a goal per game over a season at this level.

Three minutes into the second half, Middlesbrough nearly took an undeserved lead, and, as at Everton, it was Sean Gregan who nearly gave it to them, miscuing the ball in front of his own goal, and missing the far post by a foot or so. That seemed to inspire McLaren's men, and a couple of minutes later they carved out another chance, but Ehiogu, unmarked eight yards out, headed hopelessly over the bar.

In the 52nd minute, Albion should have scored. When Koumas crossed, Gregan had a free header, and when it was blocked, inadvertedly, by Lee Hughes, Gregan got the ball back and sent in a screamer that somehow missed the target.

Minutes later, the crowd erupted as if at a Cup Final, when Hughes lost his footing in the box, and the referee pointed to the penalty spot – or so they thought – as he gave the most dramatic goal kick in the history of the game! That was Hughes' last touch. He had at least put the work in, but still looks absolutely awful compared to his best. On came Dichio, back in favour with a desperate manager.

In the 73rd minute Dichio scored his first Premiership goal since January 1 2001. Two crosses came over from Neil Clement on the left; the second caused a scrimmage, from which Siggy hooked in a shot that hit Darren Moore, and then, when the fall fell kindly, **DICHIO** rapped it into the back of the net from close range. A fortunate but very deserved goal.

Nine minutes from time, as Boro came out of their shell at last, Job got up well to crash a splendid header against the bar. Unfortunately he also smacked his head against that of Moore. Both went down as if poleaxed. Darren was the lucky one, wondering off in a dazed state – Job was convulsing on the pitch, and had to be rushed to hospital for a brain scan.

That reduced Boro, who had used their three subs, to ten men, but, amazingly, they hit the bar again, substitute Noel Whelan looping a clever flicked header over Hoult in the third of the six extra minutes allocated at the end of the game. The win pulled Albion over Sunderland and out of the relegation zone.

*Attendance: 35,958*
*Referee: Alan Wiley (Burntwood)*
*Assistants: P Sharp & D C Richards*

# TOTTENHAM 3    ALBION 1

*Ziege 4, Keane 29, Poyet 79*    *Dobie 70*

| Kasey KELLER | 13-01 | Russell HOULT |
|---|---|---|
| Stephen CARR | 02-02 | Igor BALIS |
| Christian ZIEGE | 23-03 | Neil CLEMENT |
| Dean RICHARDS | 36-04 | Derek McINNES |
| Ledley KING [64] | 26-07 | Ronnie WALLWORK |
| Chris PERRY | 06-17 | Larus SIGURDSSON |
| Darren ANDERTON | 07-14 | Sean GREGAN |
| Jamie REDKNAPP | 15-11 | Jason ROBERTS [80] |
| Simon DAVIES | 29-19 | Lee HUGHES [55] |
| Teddy SHERINGHAM [73] | 10-10 | Andy JOHNSON [84] |
| Robbie KEANE | 22-18 | Jason KOUMAS |
| Steffen IVERSEN [64] | 16-23 | Adam CHAMBERS [84] |
| Gustavo POYET [73] | 14-12 | Scott DOBIE [55] |
| Les FERDINAND | 09-09 | Daniel DICHIO [80] |
| Gary DOHERTY | 12-22 | James CHAMBERS |
| Lars HIRSCHFIELD | 24-31 | Joe MURPHY |

## THE MATCH IN BRIEF

In their first visit to White Hart Lane in sixteen years (last time out, lost 0-5) Albion comprehensively outplay Spurs, but still down heavily in north London for a second time

## THE BUILD-UP

*Saturday November 30*: Alan Ashman, one of the few Albion managers to have won a trophy with the club, and a real footballing gentleman, dies age 74.

*Friday*: Albion test out three triallists; former Chelsea defender Bernard Lambourde, Artim Sakiri and Polish defender Kaczorowski. Meanwhile, reserve winger Matt Turner joins Danish side Helfolge.

## THE GAME

Spurs' first goal went in after just 200 seconds of the game; a Sigurdsson was at fault to start with, needlessly bringing down the aging Sheringham, who was doing nothing special on the edge of the box. The second culprit was Neil Clement – who was generally poor again, yet could have had a hat-trick! He did his usual trick at the free kick, of moving in and out to play offside. Had he stopped on the post, he would have stopped the low shot from **ZIEGE**, which crept just inside, with Hoult stationary.

Yet after that dreadful start, Albion dominated a dark and damp evening in North London, all for no reward. In the eighth minute, a great break down the right ended with a low Hughes cross that Johnson failed to connect with by a matter of inches at the far post. Three minutes later, another break down the same side ended with Roberts actually rounding Keller, but chipping the ball across goal from an acute angle. Then game a golden opportunity, again generated from a break down the right, but when Balis pulled the ball back perfectly, Lee Hughes missed it and Clement, coming in late, steered the ball past the post from the edge of the six yard box.

The game continued in that vein for some time, with Jason Koumas a revelation, looking worth all of the £2.5m that was paid for him, at last. He was awesome, setting up attack after attack but, as so often this season, there is no end-product. Throughout Lee Hughes was a mere cipher, and can no longer expect to get a start in favour of Dobie, who had a great 35 minutes.

The possession tally was 53-47 in favour of the Albion in the first half, but all their good work was wasted with a simple chip down the middle in the 29th minute. Robbie **KEANE** outpaced Sean Gregan, with whom he had already had several altercations, and ran clear to poke the ball over Hoult. He then ran from one side of the pitch to the other to do his somersault right in front of the Albion fans, who had been baiting in for his Wolves connections from the start.

The second goal made no difference to the pattern of the game; Albion resumed control, and Clement had three shots just off target, and Koumas put in another cracker, yet they could so easily have been three down at the break, as Keane once more streaked clear, only to be thwarted by an absolutely brilliant point blank stop by Hoult.

After a quiet start to the second half, Megson brought on Dobie for Hughes, and even Megson must have noticed the difference. In the 65th minute came the deciding moment of the game, when Dobie ran through onto a delightful Koumas chip. Out came Keller, and took him out on the edge of the box – but only got a yellow, so he was still in between the posts to save Koumas' low free kick. A disgrace – again!

Even so, Albion were soon right back in it again, in the 70th minute, when **DOBIE** capitalised on some good aggressive work by McInnes, picked his spot, and slammed in a magnificent low shot from 25 yards. In the 77th minute, Clement was given a free header from Koumas' corner, and put it past the post. The ball went straight down the other end, and Sigurdsson did well to head another own goal attempt from Gregan off his own line.

In the 79th minute, Spurs propelled a long throw into the area, and after a catalogue of hacks and miskicks, **POYET** steered the ball into the net from a yard out, to make the scoreline a real travesty of justice. The third goal finally knocked the stuffing out of the Baggies, and they played out time in what had been their classiest display of the season so far.

*Attendance: 40,391*
*Referee: Mike Dean (The Wirral)*
*Assistants: G Beale & S Gagen*

# ASTON VILLA 2    ALBION 1

*Vassell 16, Hitzlberger 90+1*        *Koumas 29*

| Peter ENCKELMAN | 13-01 | Russell HOULT |
|---|---|---|
| Olof MELLBERG | 02-02 | Igor BALIS |
| Steve STAUNTON ☐ | 23-03 | Neil CLEMENT |
| Gareth BARRY | 36-04 | Derek McINNES |
| Oyvind LEONHARDSEN | 26-07 | Darren MOORE |
| Ronny JOHNSEN | 06-17 | Sean GREGAN |
| Jlloyd SAMUEL | 07-14 | Larus SIGURDSSON |
| Lee HENDRIE | 15-11 | Jason ROBERTS [83] |
| Dion DUBLIN | 29-19 | Lee HUGHES [58] |
| Darius VASSELL | 10-10 | Andy JOHNSON |
| Thomas HITZLBERGER | 22-18 | Jason KOUMAS |
| Juan Pablo ANGEL | 16-23 | Ronnie WALLWORK |
| Stefan POSTMA | 14-12 | Scott DOBIE [83] |
| Marcus ALLBACK | 09-09 | Daniel DICHIO [58] |
| Ulises DE LA CRUZ | 12-22 | Adam CHAMBERS |
| Mark KINSELLA | 24-31 | Joe MURPHY |

**THE MATCH IN BRIEF**
Albion are unlucky, in they go down to an injury time winner at
Villa Park, but to be truthful, Villa should have won the game long
before Thomas Hitzlberger's strike.

### THE BUILD-UP

*Thursday December 12*: Darren Moore will be fit for Saturday despite his head injury

### THE GAME

In the seventh minute Hendrie went on a fantastic run, before setting up Barry to fire a powerful shot just wide. Three minutes later Vassell had a shot blocked on the line by McInnes, which precipitated a series of scrambles in the Albion box, with Gregan hacking the final effort away. Then Leonardsen had a header caught just under the bar by Hoult; from his kick Albion had their first opportunity, as Roberts streaked away to shoot hopelessly into the side-netting.

In the 16th minute, McInnes upended Hitzlberger, and Roberts got himself booked – and the ball advanced 10 yards into the 'D' of the area — for arguing. Hitzlberger fired his shot into the wall, but it dropped perfectly at the feet of **VASSELL**, who rolled it into the net.

As the rain began to fall, Villa continued to run the show, with Barry's speculative long ranger flashing inches wide and, in the 22nd minute, Hoult doing really well to flip backwards to palm out a great long range header by Dublin.

Then Albion started to play, and with Koumas having a great game, we started to look as if we had a chance. It was the Welsh international who levelled in the 29th minute. Good work by McInnes and Johnson let in Hughes; his feeble shot was blocked, but it fell for **KOUMAS**, who cleverly picked his shot to sidefoot home from just on the edge of the area, his first goal in the stripes.

The goal deflated the home side, and Albion started to make some chances, with Hughes and Roberts both shooting over. Even so, right on the break Hendrie sent in a fantastic shot from 25 yards that Hoult got the faintest of touches to, to deflect it onto the bar, and back out – another great save.

Both Hendrie and Vassell went close to adding to the Villa score early in the second half, whilst Gregan had to look sharp to scramble away a far post effort from Dublin. In the 58th minute Dichio was introduced, and immediately got into a barney with Staunton, who had to be warned by the referee. ten minutes later, Staunton elbowed the Albion man in the chest – he went down and Staunton went off, having already been booked for dissent in the first half.

Albion sat back to play for the point. Villa's ten men always looked the side more likely to score, with Hoult saving brilliantly from Vassell's fierce shot, and Sigurdsson back-heading against his own post – but then again, Albion should have had an 81st minute penalty when Johnsen blatantly pushed Roberts in the back in the area. Just when it looked as if the point had been won, a minute or so into injury time, **HITZL-BERGER** unleashed a shot out of the blue, from fully 25 yards, that took a deflection to loop over another gallant attempt at a save from Hoult. You didn't have to be claret and blue to realise that they deserved it...

*Jason Koumas records his first Albion goal with a classic strike at Villa Park*

*Attendance: 26,703*
*Referee: Clive Wilkes (Gloucester)*
*Assistants: D Bryan & N Bannister*

# ALBION 2          # SUNDERLAND 2
*Dichio 27, Koumas 32*          *Phillips 56, 64*

| Russell HOULT | 01-01 | Jurgen MACHO |
|---|---|---|
| Igor BALIS [65] | 02-15 | Stephen WRIGHT |
| Neil CLEMENT | 03-30 | Phil BABB |
| Derek McINNES | 04-04 | Jody CRADDOCK |
| Darren MOORE | 05-06 | George McCARTNEY [HT] |
| Sean GREGAN | 14-12 | Paul THIRWELL |
| Jason KOUMAS | 18-14 | Kevin KILBANE |
| Jason ROBERTS [65] | 11-07 | Gavin McCANN |
| Andy JOHNSON | 10-16 | Michael GRAY |
| Daniel DICHIO | 19-11 | Kevin PHILLIPS |
| Larus SIGURDSSON | 17-09 | Tore Andre FLO |
| Scott DOBIE [65] | 12-28 | David BELLION [HT] |
| Adam CHAMBERS [65] | 22-08 | Joachim BJORKLAND |
| Lee HUGHES | 09-13 | Michael INGHAM |
| Ronnie WALLWORK | 07-35 | Marcus STEWART |
| Joe MURPHY | 31-31 | Michael PROCTOR |

**THE MATCH IN BRIEF**
A key result in a traumatic season. A win would have taken Albion out of the bottom three for Christmas, but they allow a two goal lead to slip against fellow strugglers Sunderland

### THE BUILD-UP

*Monday December 16*: Phil Gilchrist has an ankle injury that will put him out of the entire Christmas programme.

*Wednesday*: Albion president, Sir Bert Millichip, dies, aged 88.

### THE GAME

Sergeant Wilko's Black Cats met Sergeant-major Megson's Baggies; it was the Premiership Cup Final, as far as both sides were concerned, with the winners out of the bottom three for Christmas. Dichio started the game for the first time since Man United, leaving the hopelessly out of touch Hughes as sub.

Sunderland opened very brightly, and could easily have taken the lead in the first few minutes. First Flo was allowed too much time to cut in from the left, to curl in a shot that Hoult just managed to touch onto the post for a corner. From the flag-kick, McCann's 20 yard shot was turned away in some style by the in-form keeper.

Having weathered that early storm, Albion took over, and dominated, without being able to break through a Sunderland side that was defending far too deeply.

The breakthrough came in the 27th minute when Koumas, who was having a third consecutive top quality outing, placed a corner perfectly onto the head of former Sunderland man Daniel **DICHIO**, and he put it home with a imperious flick of his head. Albion poured forward confidently after that, and scored a second five minutes later. Roberts was brought down on the edge of the area, and with all of us expecting a Clement rocket to ping off row LL in the Brummie Road, **KOUMAS** nipped in first and curled a glorious shot into the top corner, leaving Macho helpless.

The visitors should have pulled a goal back in the 39th minute, when Balis' horrendously weak back pass was intercepted by Flo, but the ex-Chelsea man, having rounded Hoult, passed to Michael Gray, who shot feebly wide. Wilkinson went for broke in the second half, by bringing on speedy Frenchman David Bellion, and how he tormented Clement down the right. It was from his cross that Kevin Kilbane flashed a header wide, as Sunderland showed some early promise, but their spirit had buckled – this looked odds on an easy win for the Albion.

Until... step forward Sean Gregan. In the 56th minute an innocuous long ball got Gregan in all sorts of trouble, and he allowed Kevin **PHILLIPS** to run in, nick the ball, and lift it over Hoult.

After that, Albion were a shambles. They completely lost their shape, not helped by the removal of Roberts immediately after the second Sunderland goal. That came just eight minutes later, when Sigurdsson – who also had a stinker – allowed **PHILLIPS** to cut in from the left wing, to crash home a low shot past Hoult into the corner, from twenty yards. Earlier, we had had a narrow escape when Moore had got in the way of a goal-bound Thirwell effort.

After that, there could only be one winner – but it seemed as if Sunderland we happy enough with one unexpected point, and didn't press for the rest. fortunately. That allowed Albion more of the play than their shaky form deserved, and because of that, they nearly snatched an 88th minute winner, when Koumas placed another great corner, only for Andy Johnson, with a free header three yards out, to wave his coiffure at it, and miss. It was just as well that Bolton, West Ham and Leeds all drew.

*A second consecutive goal from Koumas*

*Attendance: 27,025*
*Referee: Graham Poll (Herts)*
*Assistants: P Canadine & G Atkins*

# ALBION 1      ARSENAL 2

*Dichio 3*        *Jeffers 48, Henry 83*

| | | |
|---|---|---|
| Russell HOULT | 01-01 | David SEAMAN |
| Adam CHAMBERS [84] | 23-03 | Ashley COLE |
| Neil CLEMENT | 03-23 | Sol CAMPBELL |
| Ronnie WALLWORK [81] | 07-05 | Martin KEOWN |
| Darren MOORE | 05-12 | LAUREN |
| Sean GREGAN | 14-04 | Patrick VIERA |
| Jason KOUMAS | 18-09 | Francis JEFFERS [68] |
| Jason ROBERTS | 11-16 | Gio. BRONCKHORST [68] |
| Andy JOHNSON | 10-19 | GILBERTO |
| Daniel DICHIO | 09-11 | Sylvian WILTORD [79] |
| Larus SIGURDSSON | 17-14 | Thierry HENRY |
| Scott DOBIE [84] | 12-25 | KANU [68] |
| James CHAMBERS [81] | 22-07 | Robert PIRES [68] |
| Lee HUGHES | 19-28 | Kolo TOURE [79] |
| Igor BALIS | 02-20 | Matthew UPSON |
| Joe MURPHY | 31-41 | Craig HOLLOWAY |

### THE MATCH IN BRIEF
Against all the odds, amid an outbreak of dislocated shoulders,
Albion push Arsenal to the limit, only to go down to a real
poacher's goal from Thierry Henry

## THE BUILD-UP

*Saturday December 21:* Before the game with Sunderland, there is a minute's silence for Alan Ashman, Sir Bert Millichip and Arthur Rowley.

*Tuesday 24*: It's an unhappy Christmas for the Baggies. Following on from Jordao's dislocated shoulder in training, Derek McInnes suffers the same injury, going for a diving header...

## THE GAME

There was some dispiriting talk amongst the fans before this game. And more than once, the Albion's record home defeat was mentioned – never have Albion been beaten by more than five clear goals at home in a League game. But put together Arsenal in top form, and Albion in the sort of form that they showed in the second half against Sunderland, and who knows what might have happened.

As it did happen, Albion started against Arsenal like a team possessed. Derek McInnes was out, with a dislocated shoulder suffered in training, and Balis was dropped, after a series of poor games, Wallwork and Adam Chambers coming in, but the rearranged side burst off the starting block to terrorise the champions and League leaders. They had a corner under their belts after just ten seconds. After fifty seconds, Dichio had had a superb 25 yard shot tipped over by Seaman.

After 150 seconds, Albion were a goal up, when Koumas flighted another one of those tempting corners, which **DICHIO** bulleted home from inside the six yard box. Sensation, as the teleprinters spewed the news all over the country. Could it be our first home win against the Gunners in nearly thirty years?

Well, not if Arsenal could help it. They went straight into the attack, and Chambers had to hack the ball away after it had travelled right across the Albion goal line. Twice Sol Campbell sent feeble headers wide from corners, as Arsenal camped in the Albion half, and sprayed

the ball around. Wiltord skinned Chambers, but his cross drifted too close to Hoult, who had to tip it over, and Henry had a couple of good openings, but, fortunately, he had a real stinker of a game, and did nothing with them. Against all the odds, Albion kept their clean sheet up to the break, but it was hard to see them lasting another 45 minutes.

As it was, they lasted just three. Arsenal came out fighting, and within a minute Hoult saved brilliantly when he tipped over Bronckhorst's shot, then Henry fired a free kick into the wall. In the 48th minute, though, the game was up, when Cole crossed from the left, the defence failed to cut it out, and **JEFFERS** nipped in, five yards out, to lift the ball over Hoult.

There was a rapid response from the Albion, who did not seem too disheartened, as Sigurdsson headed inches over the bar from another Koumas corner. Then, in the 77th minute, came the chance of glory, when Dichio headed on from Gregan's long clearance. Roberts got the ball, in the same position as he had scored from at Highbury. Once again he completely bamboozled Keown, and sent him sprawling, only to clip the shot across Seaman, and against the inside of the far post, and back out, where Dichio, following up, just missed connecting. Tragic.

Two minutes later this end to end encounter threw up another chance, when Henry missed, what was for him, an absolute sitter, steering the ball over the bar from close in. No matter – by now Wenger had introduced two quality subs – Kanu and Pires – and they went for the kill. What a shame the goal came from a fluke, seven minutes from time, when Adam Chambers' routine clearance was charged down. The ball looped into the air, and fell perfectly for **HENRY**, who brought it down well, and fired across Hoult for what, in the end, was a deserved winner, if only for the quality of the football – as opposed to sheer grit and guts – that Arsenal displayed throughout.

*Attendance: 26,196*
*Referee: Steve Dunn (Bristol)*
*Assistants: A Green & K Woolmer*

# CHARLTON A. 1    ALBION 0
*Lisbie 6*

| Dean KIELEY | 01-01 | Russell HOULT |
|---|---|---|
| Chris POWELL | 03-23 | Adam CHAMBERS [72] |
| Richard RUFUS | 05-03 | Neil CLEMENT |
| Mark FISH [52] | 06-07 | Ronnie WALLWORK |
| Scott PARKER [78] | 26-07 | Darren MOORE |
| jason EUELL | 09-14 | Sean GREGAN |
| Claus JENSEN | 10-17 | Larus SIGURDSSON |
| Gary ROWETT | 15-11 | Jason ROBERTS |
| Shaun BARTLETT [64] | 17-09 | Daniel DICHIO |
| Luke YOUNG | 19-10 | Andy JOHNSON |
| Kevin LISBIE | 23-18 | Jason KOUMAS [81] |
| Jonathan FORTUNE [52] | 24-06 | Phil GILCHRIST |
| Chris BART-WILLIAMS [78] | 16-12 | Scott DOBIE [72] |
| Jonatan JOHANSSON [64] | 21-19 | Lee HUGHES [81] |
| Ben ROBERTS | 22-22 | James CHAMBERS |
| Paul KONCHESKY | 18-31 | Joe MURPHY |

**THE MATCH IN BRIEF**
Albion go down to an eighth defeat in ten away games, but it is difficult to fathom out why. They complete dominate the game against Charlton, yet still go down 1-0...

## THE BUILD-UP

*Friday December 27:* There are no further injury problems for Saturday's game against in-form Charlton Athletic at The Valley. Phil Gilchrist is expected to return on the bench.

## THE GAME

Albion had just one win in fifteen behind them, following the Boxing Day defeat against Arsenal. Charlton, who are all too often quoted as the example that aspiring Premiership clubs need to follow, were unbeaten in seven games since November 9, having recently accounted for Liverpool, Leeds and Manchester City, but fresh from a disastrous second half at White Hart Lane, where they had thrown away a two goal lead.

As the game got off to a frantic start, you could see why they had begun to leak goals. In the first minute Andy Johnson was through, only to have the ball snatched off his toes as he was about to shoot. Sixty seconds later, Chambers' cross from the right beat the defence, and Roberts pulled the ball down, expertly beat two men in the turn – then decided he wanted to beat two more, and after the unnecessary delay, hit his shot straight at Kieley, 25 yards out.

We were still not finished; in the third minute a Dichio flick let in Roberts again, but this time, close in on goal, a defender managed to boot the ball off his toe.

With Albion's thrilling opening burst satiated, it was the home side's turn. In the fifth minute Moore fouled Bartlett 25 yards out, and Hoult brilliantly tipped over Rowett's free kick that was arrowing its way into the corner. From the throw-in that resulted from the corner, Euell had just Hoult to beat, two feet out, but the next England keeper – surely – somehow managed to instinctively block the shot.

From the corner, though, Hoult blotted his copybook, attempting to beat **LISBIE** to the punch at the near post, and failing, allowing the Charlton man to head home from a yard out.

Then, to complete a hat-trick of remarkable saves, in the eleventh minute, Hoult was there again to tip a low shot around the post after Parker had been criminally allowed to run seventy yards with the ball, to the edge of the box.

And that, for Charlton, was that. Remarkably, Albion controlled the game from then on, creating chance after chance in what was their best performance of the season so far – but they just could not get the ball into the net...

On 19 minutes Jason Koumas' low 25 yard free kick beat the wall, but hit the bottom of the post. Then, after Dichio and Johnson had had shots blocked, Moore was the unlucky on the half hour mark, when his powerful header from a great Koumas corner was headed off the line by Parker. Even Ronnie Wallwork got in the act in first half injury time, racing forward to send in a low shot that Kieley, at full stretch, just managed to push the ball round the upright.

The 'rout' continued after the break, with Adam Chambers poking the ball over the bar, and Moore heading another Koumas corner inches wide. Two minutes after that, it was Dichio's turn, Rufus clearing his header off the line. Everything was coming through Koumas; you just didn't want anybody else to have the ball, he was so good. In the 58th minute, Dichio was there again, with Parker booting his effort off the line.

In the 68th minute came yet another dreadful decision, when Roberts was hauled to the ground by Rufus; a clear penalty, but the referee did nothing, and the move ended with Clement hammering the loose ball just wide, after which the official was surrounded by a crowd of very angry Albion players.

That soured the game somewhat, and it wound down with a series of niggling bookings, but even at the death Albion were looking for goals, with Scott Dobie slamming a beautiful shot off the top of the bar in injury time.

*Attendance: 19,909*
*Referee:  David Elleray (Harrow)*
*Assistants: D Babski & G Sutton*

# ALBION 3　　BRADFORD C. 1
*Dichio 4, 11, 19*　　　*Danks 79*

| Albion | | Bradford C. |
|---|:---:|---|
| Russell HOULT | 01-17 | Aiden DAVISON |
| Adam CHAMBERS | 23-14 | Gus UHLENBEEK |
| Neil CLEMENT | 03-22 | Wayne JACOBS |
| Ronnie WALLWORK [85] | 07-12 | Robert MOLENAAR |
| Darren MOORE | 05-06 | Mark BOWER |
| Sean GREGAN [HT] | 14-18 | Lewis EMANUEL |
| Jason KOUMAS | 18-16 | Michael STANDING |
| Jason ROBERTS [HT] | 11-19 | Claus JORGENSEN |
| Andy JOHNSON | 10-34 | Simon FRANCIS |
| Daniel DICHIO | 09-11 | Andy GRAY |
| Larus SIGURDSSON | 17-15 | JUANJO [56] |
| Scott DOBIE [HT] | 12-35 | Mark DANKS [56] |
| James CHAMBERS | 22-38 | Danny FORREST |
| Phil GILCHRIST [HT] | 19-10 | Paul EVANS |
| Igor BALIS [85] | 02-24 | Paul REID |
| Brian JENSEN | 21-36 | Nicholas BEACH |

## THE MATCH IN BRIEF
Although Bradford City have had a good run of late, their mix of
youngsters and older heads is no match for Albion, for whom
Daniel Dichio gets  a fifteen minute hat-trick

## THE BUILD-UP

*Tuesday December 31:* Problems for tomorrow's opponents, Fulham, who are without Hayles, Inamoto, van der Saar, Clark and Boa Morte.

*Wednesday January 1:* The Fulham game, at Loftus Road, is called off because of a waterlogged pitch.

## THE GAME

Potentially, this could well have been a tricky tie, for Bradford City's band of kids and crocks had won three of their previous four games, including a splendid 2-1 win in Wolverhampton.

The excitement started early. In the second minute a long Neil Clement ball easily split the Bradford defence, but Roberts was too casual, allowing a defender to take the ball off him. That sloppiness in the visitors' defence was to be apparent all afternoon, and two minutes later Albion took advantage of it. It was the determination of Andy Johnson which won the ball in midfield, and when it was sprayed out to Adam Chambers on the right, he crossed into the middle. Clement mistimed his jump (no surprise there!) but **DICHIO** did not, and had a fairly simple header from six yards out, making it four goal, one in each of his last four home games.

Sixty seconds later, Roberts shimmied his way into the area, only to go to ground; David Elleray decided that he had dived, rather than been fouled by Bower, and booked him, a decision that would influence the second half of the game.

No mind; in the 11th minute, it was two nil. Once again, Albion had Johnson to thank for the build-up, in which Clement won a corner, and when that was not properly cleared, Wallwork whipped the ball in fiercely from the left and **DICHIO** was there again, grievously unmarked, to glance a header into the corner. All five of his Hawthorns goals had been scored with his head...

That would change in the 19th minute, thanks to Jason Roberts, who burst out of midfield on one of those famous runs that look marvellous, but usually end with him shooting over the bar. This time he bewildered five men, before being crowded out, but this time, for once, he had the sense to poke the ball to **DICHIO**, who coolly side-footed the ball across Davison, and into the corner, to complete his hat-trick. It was the first such in an FA Cup tie for the Albion since Kevin Donovan troubled Aylesbury in 1992. Would this be another 8-0? Bradford were such a shambles that the Brummie Road were chanting "Sunday League" – and with good reason. They were as bad a side as were Portsmouth at The Hawthorns this time last year, and they were lucky only to lose 5-0!

Albion continued to push forward, with Roberts always a terror. Dichio had a shot blocked by a defender – that would have had us all rushing for the record books, for the last time somebody scored four in the Cup – and Koumas whipped the loose ball across an unguarded goal, then Bower tripped Roberts one-on-one, when he looked likely to score, but got away without even being booked.

At the interval, Megson took off Roberts, because of his booking, and gave Gilchrist his first run-out after injury, in place of Gregan, ready for his return, in place of Wallwork, against United net week. Sensible moves, but disastrous, as it proved, for the game. What a terrible second half it was!

Albion created just two more decent chances, both in the space of a couple of minutes. First, on 54 minutes, a perfect through ball from Wallwork found Andy Johnson, but Davison tipped his shot round the post (although none of the officials saw the touch, and gave a goal kick). Then Koumas fed Clement and he put over a fast low cross, only for Dobie to sidefoot wide from six yards.

In the 79th minute, Claus Jorgensen smashed in a great shot from thirty yards that beat Hoult all ends up, bounced back down off the underside of the bar, and fell nicely for substitute **DANKS** to head home from six yards.

*Attendance: 27,129*
*Referee: Neale Barry (Lincs)*
*Assistants: R Booth & K Stroud*

# ALBION 1            MANCHESTER U. 3
*Koumas 6*              *van Nistelroy 7, Scholes 22, Solskjaer 55*

| | | |
|---|---|---|
| Russell HOULT | 01-17 | Fabian BARTHEZ |
| Adam CHAMBERS [86] | 23-14 | Gary NEVILLE |
| Neil CLEMENT | 03-22 | Phil NEVILLE |
| Ronnie WALLWORK | 07-12 | Rio FERDINAND |
| Darren MOORE | 05-06 | Roy KEANE [81] |
| Phil GILCHRIST | 14-18 | Danny SILVESTRE |
| Jason KOUMAS | 18-16 | Wes BROWN |
| Jason ROBERTS | 11-19 | David BECKHAM |
| Andy JOHNSON | 10-34 | Paul SCHOLES |
| Daniel DICHIO | 09-11 | Ruud VAN NISTELROY |
| Larus SIGURDSSON[75] | 17-15 | Ole G SOLSKJAER[67] |
| Scott DOBIE [75] | 12-35 | John O'SHEA [81] |
| James CHAMBERS | 22-38 | Diego FORLAN [67] |
| Derek McINNES | 19-10 | Laurent BLANC |
| Igor BALIS [86] | 02-24 | RICARDO |
| Joe MURPHY | 31-36 | Kieran RICHARDSON |

**THE MATCH IN BRIEF**
As the Manchester United circus rolls into town, ALbion are out-
classed, despite taking a sixth minute lead through Jason Koumas;
they hold the lead for 22 seconds, and lose 3-1

## THE BUILD-UP

*Monday January 6* Albion get a reasonable draw in the fourth round of the FA Cup; away to First Division Watford.

*Tuesday*: With the January transfer window wide open, Albion have already missed out on Spartak Moscow's Vladimir Beschastnyk, who looks set for Fernbache. CSKA Sofia want £1m for Artim Sakiri, so that move also looks in doubt.

## THE GAME

On a cold but sunny day in January, the biggest show in football came to West Bromwich, giving the biggest gate of the season, and bringing with it its crowd of hangers-on – unbelievably, a couple of hundred snarling United 'fans' had to be escorted away from the ground at 2.55, by police kitted up with riot gear. After the game, it was impossible to get off the club car park because of the crowds milling around the United coach in Halfords Lane, looking for autographs. And there were reports of forged tickets, for the first time in years. Add to that the fighting before, during and after the game, and it was just like 'the old days!'

But to the game. Well, Albion were in it for twenty minutes, anyway. In the fifth minute Solskjaer controlled a long ball from Keane – who had survived a hamstring scare – and actually rounded Hoult on the right, but the ball took a bad bounce, and went out for a goal kick.

Then, in the sixth minute, the side repeated the ecstasy of the Arsenal game, when they took a shock lead. The goal was down to a shocking crossfield ball by Rio Ferdinand, who put the ball straight to **KOUMAS**. He ran forty yards, with the defenders backing off, before, from 25 yards, belting the ball into the corner of the net. Wonderful – and The Hawthorns erupted as if it was the F A Cup Final.

They held the lead for all of half a minute. This time, it was an even worse mistake by Neil Clement – that should see him dropped, to be honest – that caused it. He had plenty of time to clear on the left,

but, a few yards outside he tried to dummy David Beckham, ran the ball into him, and after that it was a simple procedure for Mr Spice to whip a cross in for **VAN NISTEL-ROY** to poke the ball through Hoult's legs from four yards out. Shocking!

Four minutes later, Scholes charged down a Sigurdsson clearance, and put the ball into the middle, but fortunately his cross fell badly for van Nistelroy, who swung and missed the ball. Then Keane had a screamer from 25 yards that Hoult could only watch as it went just wide. It was beginning to look as if the early goal had been the worst thing we could have done.

Indeed, in the 16th minute, Solskjaer should have scored, but eight yards out, and unmarked, he headed wide from Scholes' cross. It was all United, and they went into the lead in the 22nd minute, with a elementary goal from the training ground. Van Nistelroy put Keane in down the right with a one-two, and the Irish thug took the ball to the byline before crossing in low for **SCHOLES** to take the ball early, on the volley, before a defender had moved.

And after that, to be frank, it really was like a training session – you know, the sort Bobby Robson used to organise for England, against the likes of Aylesbury. The gulf in class was hard to stomach, if you had been a fan when we regularly used to thrash United in the Sixties and Seventies…

At least, in the second half, Albion were less respectful of United, and got stuck in a bit, but it was still awful to watch. Straight away Scholes was inches wide from a Beckham short corner, and they extended their lead in the 55th minute. Gary Neville put over the cross from the right, van Nistelroy missed it, but **SOLSKJAER** was there, unmarked, to shoot home high into the top corner, a marvellous piece of cool finishing.

In the 72nd minute, there was a rare shot on target from the Albion, when Barthez had to get his shorts dirty to save Koumas' 35 yard dipping volley. Out broke United, five on two, and when van Nistelroy put in Beckham on the right, Hoult had to make another great save.

*Attendance: 39,708*
*Referee: Uriah Rennie (Sheffield)*
*Assistants: A Butler & T Kettle*

# LEEDS UNITED 0    ALBION 0

| | | |
|---|---|---|
| Paul ROBINSON | 13-01 | Russell HOULT |
| Teddy LUCIC | 15-02 | Igor BALIS [35] |
| Gary KELLY | 02-03 | Neil CLEMENT |
| Jason WILCOX [69] | 16-04 | Derek McINNES |
| Lucas RADEBE | 05-05 | Darren MOORE |
| Paul OKON [79] | 24-06 | Phil GILCHRIST |
| Dominic MATTEO | 21-14 | Sean GREGAN |
| Eirik BAKKE [69] | 19-12 | Scott DOBIE [63] |
| Harry KEWELL | 10-09 | Daniel DICHIO |
| Alan SMITH | 17-10 | Andy JOHNSON ❑ |
| Mark VIDUKA | 09-18 | Jason KOUMAS [79] |
| Seth JOHNSON [69] | 20-07 | Ronnie WALLWORK [35] |
| James MILNER [69] | 38-17 | Larus SIGURDSSON [79] |
| Robbie FOWLER [79] | 27-19 | Lee HUGHES [63] |
| Danny MILLS | 18-24 | Ifeanyi UDEZE |
| Nigel MARTYN | 01-31 | Joe MURPHY |

**THE MATCH IN BRIEF**
A rare away point for the Baggies at Leeds —but it could so easily
have been three, as Albion are denied a clear penalty after a Lucas
Radebe error

## THE BUILD-UP

*Tuesday January 14* Albion sign PAOK defender Ifeanyi Udeze on loan until the end of the season.

## THE GAME

Leeds started strongly, with the unmarked Dominic Matteo volleying across goal, and Hoult having to rush out of goal to thwart Alan Smith after Gregan (yet again) had made a serious error in misjudging the pace of the ball. In the sixth minute Russell Hoult had to make the first of several very good saves, when he saved with his legs from Viduka, whose toe-poke had caught him off balance.

Then, on fourteen minutes, there was a nasty mix-up between Gilchrist and Hoult, the former heading over the latter on the bye-line and nearly letting in Alan Smith. Sixty seconds later, though, and Albion could well have taken the lead from Clement's free kick. No, not from the kick itself – that doesn't happen any more, unfortunately – but when the ball bounced off the wall, Dobie was in there first, and shot just wide, missing a goal identical to the one that he had scored so spectacularly at Bolton this season.

The home side bounced back. In the 25th minute Hoult had to make another brilliant save, tipping round Viduka's low shot from the edge of the box. Six minutes later, Russell made an even better stop, throwing himself full length to tip round Smith's super volley.

At that point Megson withdrew the limping Balis, and replaced him with Wallwork, whose first touch was to race down the wing and put over a great cross which Dobie reached too late, and bundled into the side-netting (pictured).

The longer the game went on, in the second half, the more likely it was that Albion might even win it. Early in the second half both Clement and Koumas had good shots on goal, which, with their deflections, could have gone anywhere, before bouncing out for corners. Could Albion score? Not after Andy Johnson had picked up two bookings in the space of three minutes, no. In the 71st minute he was booked, rather harshly, for a foul on Viduka. Two minutes later Lee Hughes raced onto a long free kick. Lucas Radebe misjudged the pace of the ball, and slipped, just as Hughes nipped round him to collect. Down went Radebe, who then punched the ball away from Hughes, in the box. A clear a penalty as you could wish for, but instead, referee Rennie gave a foul against Hughes. Andy Johnson was so incensed that he gave the official a mouthful, got his second yellow, and off he went. Yet Albion could still have won it; it took a great instinctive save by Robinson, from Wallwork's volley on the edge of the box, to keep his side in it.

"I admit it. It was handball – I just lost my footing" – Lucas Radebe after the game

*Scott Dobie goes close at Elland Road, as Albion grab a useful point from crisis-stricken Leeds United*

*Attendance: 16,975*
*Referee: Jeff Winter (Stockton-on-Tees)*
*Assistants: B D Baker & N Bannister*

# WATFORD 1       ALBION 0

*Helguson 80*

| | | |
|---|---|---|
| Alec CHAMBERLAIN | 01-01 | Russell HOULT |
| Neal ARDLEY [88] | 02-07 | Ronnie WALLWORK |
| Paul ROBINSON | 03-03 | Neil CLEMENT |
| Paolo VERNAZZA | 04-04 | Derek McINNES [56] |
| Neil COX | 05-05 | Darren MOORE [83] |
| Allan NIELSEN | 07-06 | Phil GILCHRIST |
| Micah HYDE | 08-14 | Sean GREGAN |
| Tommy SMITH | 09-11 | Jason ROBERTS [66] |
| Heidar HELGUSON [87] | 18-09 | Daniel DICHIO |
| Marcus GAYLE | 27-10 | Andy JOHNSON |
| Jermaine PENNANT | 29-18 | Jason KOUMAS |
| Gavin MAHON [88] | 12-23 | Adam CHAMBERS [83] |
| Gifton NOEL-WILLIAMS[87] | 15-17 | Larus SIGURDSSON [56] |
| Anthony McNAMEE | 16-12 | Scott DOBIE [66] |
| Wayne BROWN | 10-24 | Ifeanyi UDEZE |
| Richard LEE | 30-31 | Joe MURPHY |

**THE MATCH IN BRIEF**
The low point in the season, as Albion bow out of the FA Cup with barely a fight, beaten by a very average First Division Watford side (who go on to the semi-final!) at Vicarage Road

## THE BUILD-UP

*Monday January 20* It is confirmed that Andy Johnson will only miss one game as a result of his two yellow cards at Leeds.

*Tuesday*: Albion are turned down by US defender Tony Sanneh, whilst Tottenham's Tim Sherwood is contemplating joining First Division leaders Portsmouth, rather that the Baggies.

*Thursday*: And now it's no-go for two more players, Roberto Rios and Salva Ballesta, but Megson is hoping to go back to CSKA Sofia with a new offer for Macedonian Sakiri. Time is running out for the transfer window, which closes at the end of the month...

## THE GAME

There is little doubt that the season reached its nadir at Vicarage Road – at least, we hope it did, because it is difficult to contemplate something worse that this.

As is so often, it wasn't the defeat itself, painful as it was to go out of the Cup so early, with so many Premier sides already out – it was the manner of the defeat. Not once in the ninety-four minutes of play did Albion force a save out of Chamberlain. It was not until referee Jeff Winter put the final whistle to his mouth that Sean Gregan sent in a testing shot, that the keeper fielded, with some difficulty, but, of course, it would not have counted had it gone in.

It had looked so much better at the start. In the first minute Moore at least got a weak header on target from a free kick, and two minutes later Roberts got away onto a lob from Dichio, and should have done better than he did before being crowded out.

Watford started to dominate the game after the first twenty minutes, but never looked like scoring a goal. Of course, neither did the Albion... On the right, on-loan Arsenal junior Jermaine Pennant was skinning Clement at will, and the former Chelsea youngster badly needs a rest.

The most interesting action of the first half was a bizarre incident in the 33rd minute, when Gregan appeared to push Neilsen, in an off-the-ball incident, in the back; in turn, he cannoned into the back of Hoult's head, and the keeper was down, needing several minutes' treatment. There was a flash of the real Jason Roberts six minutes before the break, when he brilliantly beat four men, before Dichio scooped the loose ball over the bar.

If the first half was bad, the second was a real disaster. Albion just went from bad to worse, ceding the entire midfield to the home side – even Koumas can't do it on his own. And now Watford were starting to look dangerous. In the 53rd minute Neilsen blasted wide from close range. Sixty seconds later, Moore blundered into Tommy Smith, in the box – a clear penalty. Neil Cox strode up to take it, and blasted hard, but Hoult brilliantly dived to his left to block, his second successive penalty save at Watford. On the hour Smith beat Sigurdsson, then Moore, who fell over, before passing to Neilsen. he should have shot, but, fortunately, he tried to set up somebody else, and Johnson was able to nick the ball away

One incident in the 72nd minute summed up the whole game. Moore put in a terrible back pass, Hoult did his best, but looped the ball into the air, Sigurdsson made a joke first time clearance, and Neilsen was in, to send in a tremendous left foot volley a foot wide of the far post.

Five minutes later Vernazza smashed a shot against the crossbar from close range, and by the 80th minute, we were out of the Cup for another year. It started with Gregan, who gifted possession, then Sigurdsson regained the ball, and gave it away again. Two quick passes, and **HELGUSON** was unmarked on the right hand side of the box, to slip the ball past Hoult.

In the 88th minute, there was a glimmer of hope, at the Albion end. Koumas slung over the free kick from the right, and there, at the far post, was Sigurdsson, who guided a powerful header across goal, off the underside of the bar, and away; but an equaliser would have been a travesty. Make no mistake about it; Albion were lucky — had they met Farnborough or Dagenham on this form, the fans would have been re-living the Woking debacle.

*Attendance: 26,113*
*Referee: Andy D'Urso (Billericay)*
*Assistants: M Tingey & C Bassindale*

# ALBION 0          CHARLTON A. 1

*Bartlett 60*

| | | |
|---|:---:|---|
| Russell HOULT | 01-01 | Dean KIELY |
| Ronnie WALLWORK | 07-02 | Radostin KISHISHEV |
| Ifeanyi UDEZE | 24-03 | Chris POWELL |
| Ronnie WALLWORK | 07-06 | Mark FISH |
| Darren MOORE [52] | 05-05 | Richard RUFUS |
| Phil GILCHRIST | 06-07 | Scott PARKER |
| Jason KOUMAS | 18-17 | Shaun BARTLETT |
| Jason ROBERTS | 11-24 | Jonathan FORTUNE |
| Andy JOHNSON | 10-23 | Kevin LISBIE [86] |
| Daniel DICHIO [75] | 09-09 | Jason EUELL |
| Adam CHAMBERS | 23-10 | Claus JENSEN [79] |
| Scott DOBIE [75] | 12-21 | Jonatan JOHANSSON [86] |
| Larus SIGURDSSON | 17-18 | Paul KONCHESKY [79] |
| Derek McINNES [52] | 04-13 | Paul RACHUBKA |
| Neil CLEMENT | 03-16 | Chris BART-WILLIAMS |
| Joe MURPHY | 31-30 | Tahar EL KHALEJ |

### THE MATCH IN BRIEF

For the second time in the space of a month, Albion control the game against Charlton, but fail to get the ball into the net. The defeat costs them the chance to move away from relegation

## THE BUILD-UP

*Sunday January 26* Because of Fulham's victory over Charlton in the FA Cup, Albion will meet the Cottagers (at Loftus Road!) in their rearranged League game on February 19.

*Monday*: Albion have had a £1m bid for Crewe's top scorer, Rob Hulse, turned down.

*Tuesday*: Andy Johnson and jason Koumas are both called up for Wales for the home game with Bosnia-Herzogovina on February 12. Good news; both Bolton and Sunderland lose at home, which means Albion could move out of the bottom three tomorrow...

## THE GAME

On a night when the result was all important, following defeats for both Bolton and Sunderland the previous evening, Albion gave an improved display, but, once again, looked as if they did not know where the next goal is coming from. Charlton were there for the taking, and Albion had the opportunity to move out of the bottom two, with a win against a Charlton side who they had outplayed at The Valley just a few weeks ago (but lost the game 1-0). Talk about déjà vu. Albion, for all their failings, all over the pitch, dominated the game in terms of possession, but, as at Watford, hardly got a shot on target. Charlton soaked up the pressure, struck when they had the chance.

The night was marked by the debut of the only new signing of the transfer window period, Ifeanyi Udeze.

In the 15th minute Andy Johnson tried to get on the end of a loose ball in the box, but completely missed his kick, near the penalty spot. Seven minutes later, Wallwork swung in a free kick and Kevin Lisbie – who scored the only goal of the game at the Valley – was a whisker away from heading an own goal.

Down to the other end, as Gregan, who has taken up the important role vacated by Clement, of running backwards and forwards from the line at free kicks, headed Claus Jensen's 20 yard free kick off the line. There was another escape in the 32nd minute, when Darren Moore missed a back header, and leaned on Lisbie in the area to stop him getting to the ball. It could so easily have been a penalty.

It all went downhill for the Albion in the 36th minute, when they fashioned a great break down the right; Koumas put over the perfect centre, and Wallwork, unchallenged, headed for goal, only for Kiely to make a fantastic one-handed stop. The troubles continued for Megson in the 52nd minute, when Moore fell awkwardly, and was helped off the field in considerable pain, to be replaced by Derek McInnes, with Wallwork dropping back. Who knows? Perhaps Moore would have been there, eight minutes later, to cut out Jensen's free kick (conceded by an awful tackle by Gregan on Lisbie) to the far post. As it was, Shaun **BARTLETT** was able to get in a clear header, which Hoult may well have got to, had the ball not caught Dichio on the shins, to leave England's Number One completely flat-footed.

Straight from the kick off Jason Roberts – who had a terrible time, with Rufus hanging onto his arm, or his back, or his shirt, all game – went through, only to be stopped in full flight, in the box, by a tackle from Mark Fish that referee Andy D'Urso thought was OK. To be fair, it was probably D'Urso's only decent call of the night.

In the 76th minute, Charlton had their best effort on target – a back header from Gilchrist which Hoult had to tip over, just under the bar. Six minutes from time came the Baggies' last chance to level, when Gregan lofted in a cross from near the halfway line. Dobie and a defender climbed for the ball, along with Kiely. All three missed it, and the ball slammed against the post, thus denying Gregan his second fluke goal of the season.

*Attendance: 34,765*
*Referee: Neal Barry (Scunthorpe)*
*Assistants: D Bryan & R Burton*

# MANCHESTER C. 1  ALBION 2

*Gilchrist (og) 22*                    *Clement 17, Moore 72*

| | | |
|---|---|---|
| Carlo NASH | 20-01 | Russell HOULT |
| Steve HOWEY | 24-23 | Adam CHAMBERS |
| Kevin HORLOCK | 06-03 | Neil CLEMENT |
| David SOMMELL | 02-04 | Derek McINNES |
| Sylvian DISTIN | 05-05 | Darren MOORE |
| Niclas JENSEN [81] | 03-06 | Phil GILCHRIST |
| Marc-Vivien FOE | 23-14 | Sean GREGAN |
| Robbie FOWLER | 33-19 | Lee HUGHES [66] |
| Ali BENARBIA [68] | 08-11 | Jason ROBERTS ▢ |
| Richard DUNNE [HT] | 22-07 | Ronnie WALLWORK |
| Nicolas ANELKA | 39-18 | Jason KOUMAS [87] |
| Shaun GOATER [81] | 10-09 | Daniel DICHIO [66] |
| Djamel BELMADI [68] | 31-17 | Larus SIGURDSSON [87] |
| Shaun WRIGHT-PHILLIPS [HT] | 29-12 | Scott DOBIE |
| Jihai SUN | 17-20 | JORDAO |
| Nicky WEAVER | 12-31 | Joe MURPHY |

**THE MATCH IN BRIEF**
Albion overshadow Robbie Fowler's debut with a great performance in what will be their final visit to Maine Road. Defenders Clement and Moore score for Albion; Gilchrist for City...

## THE BUILD-UP

*Thursday January 24* One more, final attempt to sign Artim Sakiri from CSKA Sofia fails, and the Macedonian playmaker, who scored the dramatic goal past David Seaman last year, may well being playing AGAINST the Albion next month, for Bolton — who have already signed Slava Ballesta...

*Friday:* The transfer window closes at 6 pm, with no more new players signed.

## THE GAME

Billed as the great Robbie Fowler debut match, Albion's final visit to Maine Road – City move to the Commonwealth Stadium next season – turned out to herald the best Albion performance of a miserable season, and sent thousands of Baggies fans boinging into the cold Manchester air at the final whistle. There were surprises. Dichio was dropped, for Hughes, who had his best game of the season. Clement was back, because Udeze was ill, and Jordao, not before time, actually made it onto the bench.

The game started slowly, with a lot of slick precision passing from City, as if to show who was the better side. Yet it was Albion who nearly drew first blood in the ninth minute. Jason Koumas put over one of his famous pin-point corners, and there was the unchallenged Neil Clement – whose only goal of the season had come against City at The Hawthorns – to power in a header that Carlo Nash was very fortunate to stop with his foot. Had not Clement 'gone by the book' and headed downwards, the keeper would have had no chance.

Eight minutes later, **CLEMENT** did exactly the same thing, heading down another Koumas corner from exactly the same position. This time, the ball flew past him, and bounced upwards, high into the net. After that Neil was a revelation, almost back to the great form of last season, after almost a year in the doldrums.

It didn't take City too long to get level; five minutes, in fact when, following a short corner, Kevin Horlock clipped the ball to the far post where Phil **GILCHRIST**, under severe pressure from Marc Vivien Foe, headed past Hoult, for a stunning own goal. Coincidentally, at just about the same time, Cunningham was doing the same at the Reebok, and at the Stadium of Light, Sunderland were scoring three own goals in the space of seven minutes against Charlton. Strange days indeed...

Looking much brighter than in any game of late, Albion took the game to City, but still rarely looked like scoring. City huffed and puffed, and there were a few alarms and excursions in the Albion box, not least in the 35th minute, when Anelka netted from the rebound, after Hoult had blocked Fowler's shot – but both City men were clearly a mile offside, and the 'goal' did not count.

In the 72nd minute, Albion struck again, scoring the magical second goal in a League game for only the third time this season. A good run from McInnes won a corner, followed by a second when Moore's header was saved. This time, there was no mistake, for when the flagkick reached the far post, after a scramble, **MOORE** neatly put the ball away with his weak foot. A minute or so later, after a poor kick out by Nash, Koumas went close to scoring another with a shot that was just too high. That was the end of Albion's attacking ambitions, as they pulled back, brought on Siggy, and kicked anything that moved.

Unfortunately, Roberts got a bit too carried away, and elbowed Sommell in the chest. The linesman saw it, informed the referee, and Roberts saw red.

Twice City went close as their disgruntled fans streamed out of the ground. Gilchrist atoned for his own goal with an astonishing block in the box, then Goater put a free header powerfully over the bar. On a weird day at the bottom of the Premiership, Albion leapfrogged both Sunderland and West Ham, and Bolton's 4-2 win, whilst annoying, did serve to pull Blues back into the mire.

*Attendance: 26,933*
*Referee: David Elleray (Harrow)*
*Assistants: R Lewis & P Norman*

# ALBION 1      BOLTON W. 1

*Johnson 90+2*        *Pedersen 19*

| Russell HOULT | 01-22 | Jussi JAASKELAINEN |
|---|---|---|
| Adam CHAMBERS | 23-02 | Bernard MENDY |
| Neil CLEMENT | 03-25 | Simon CHARLTON |
| Derek McINNES [77] | 04-04 | Gudni BERGSSON |
| Darren MOORE | 05-05 | Bruno N'GOTTY |
| Phil GILCHRIST [71] | 06-16 | Ivan CAMPO |
| Jason KOUMAS | 18-11 | Ricardo GARDNER |
| Jason ROBERTS [77] | 11-08 | Per FRANDSEN |
| Sean GREGAN | 14-10 | Jay-Jay OKOCHA [85] |
| Daniel DICHIO | 09-13 | Youri DJORKAEFF [73] |
| Ronnie WALLWORK | 07-09 | Henrik PEDERSEN [80] |
| Lee HUGHES [77] | 12-18 | Pierre-Yves ANDRE [85] |
| Larus SIGURDSSON | 17-15 | Kevin NOLAN [73] |
| Andy JOHNSON [77] | 04-20 | Salva BALLESTA [80] |
| Ifeanyi UDEZE [71] | 24-24 | Anthony BARNESS |
| Joe MURPHY | 31-30 | Kevin POOLE |

### THE MATCH IN BRIEF
Just as Bolton had saved the game against Albion at the Reebok, Andy Johnson scores a vital last minute equaliser at The Hawthorns; then breaks his foot!

## THE BUILD-UP

*Wednesday February 5* Reserve midfielder Mark Briggs joins the exodus to Helfolge.

## THE GAME

After the delirium of Maine Road, came the gritty tension of a real six pointer against Bolton Wanderers at The Hawthorns. Before the game Phil Gilchrist had to have a couple of pain-killing injection in his toe, whilst Dichio was throwing up all over the place. Lovely…

The start of the game was just as frantic as you might have expected. Albion showed a little early flourish through Jason Roberts, but, to be honest, Bolton's exciting side, bolstered by the previous week's 4-2 win over Blues, looked the better bet to avoid the drop. They certainly had pace all over the pitch; after a quarter of an hour's play Pedersen skinned a hopelessly naïve Gregan on the bye-line, and it took a good clearance from Moore to keep the ball out; two minutes later Gregan took his revenge, on Gardner, and was very lucky to escape with just a lecture for a silly lunge; from the free kick Frandsen shot well over, 25 yards out.

Bolton were well on top at this point, and they took the lead in the 19th minute, following a fast break out of defence by the whippet-like Bernard Mendy. He dispossessed Koumas, then ran eighty yards before giving the ball to Djorkaeff, on the edge of the Albion box. His first time shot was pathetic – but not as pathetic as Hoult's attempt to save — he hopelessly spilled the ball to the feet of **PEDERSEN**, who had no trouble tipping the ball over the line from a couple of yards out. Albion had a shout for a penalty when Campo seemed to take out Dichio in the area in the 28th minute, but when referee David Elleray allowed play to continue, Bolton broke away again and Djorkaeff again went close.

Right on half time, Jaaskelainen got into a real mess when he kicked a routine clearance straight at Dichio. If only it had been somebody else… As it was, Dichio was too slow to get the ball out from under his feet, although the keeper had to come out and foul him. McInnes took a very quick free kick, and Ronnie Wallwork blew his chance of a first goal when he hit the ball straight at Campo, who cleared off the line. There was much discussion about whether the Finnish keeper should have been sent off, but there were clearly men behind him when he committed the foul, so his yellow card was the correct punishment

The second half was end to end stuff – but how powder-puff was the Albion attack? Gregan, who had a steadier second half, got up and tried a desperate toe-poke that his the inside of the right post, rolled BEHIND the keeper, along the line, before rolling just past the other post.

Things really got fraught in the last three minutes. First, the Dichio flick-on finally worked, letting in Hughes on the right, only for Jaaskelainen to make a fine save. The keeper kicked the ball out to Gardner, who raced away for fully ninety yards, before being stopped by a brilliant block by Hoult. Had that gone in, Albion would have seven points away from Bolton. Instead, in injury time, Gregan clipped the ball in, Darren Moore headed on, and of Hughes and **JOHNSON**, racing into the six yard box, the Welsh international stabbed the ball in, under the keeper. In the celebrations that followed, Johnson aggravated an earlier injury, breaking his foot, which will put him out for a month. An expensive price to pay for an absolutely essential goal.

*Andy Johnson scores — then breaks his foot*

*Attendance: 15,799*
*Referee: Uriah Rennie (Sheffield)*
*Assistants: R Lewis & P Norman*

# FULHAM 3     ALBION 0

*Saha 71, Wome 73*
*Malbranque pen 75*

| Fulham | | Albion |
|---|---|---|
| Maik TAYLOR | 12-01 | Russell HOULT |
| Steve FINNAN | 02-23 | Adam CHAMBERS |
| Andy MELVILLE | 04-03 | Neil CLEMENT [88] |
| Martin DJETOU | 17-04 | Derek McINNES |
| Alain GOMA [44] | 24-05 | Darren MOORE |
| Pierre WOME | 27-06 | Phil GILCHRIST |
| Junichi INAMOTO | 06-14 | Sean GREGAN |
| Steve MARLET | 07-19 | Lee HUGHES [70] |
| Facundo SAVA | 09-09 | Daniel DICHIO [79] |
| Steed MALBRANQUE [88] | 14-07 | Ronnie WALLWORK |
| Louis SAHA | 20-18 | Jason KOUMAS |
| Abdeslam OUADDOU [44] | 25-24 | Ifeanyi UDEZE [88] |
| Andrejs STOLCERS [88] | 40-17 | Larus SIGURDSSON |
| Martin HERRERA | 21-12 | Scott DOBIE [70] |
| Bjarne GOLDBAEK | 19-20 | JORDAO [79] |
| Dean LEACOCK | 39-31 | Joe MURPHY |

**THE MATCH IN BRIEF**
Three goals in five minutes, midway through the second half, send Albion to an undeserved defeat at Loftus Road; once again, missed chances in the first half cost them dear.

### THE BUILD-UP

*Monday February 10* The Albion players — with the exception of Andy Johnson, whose broken foot will keep him out for four weeks — leave for a mid-season break in Spain.

*Saturday*: No game for Albion, on fifth round FA Cup day.

*Tuesday*: Albion will be at full strength for tomorrow's game against Fulham, with the exception of the injured Johnson, and suspended Jason Roberts.

### THE GAME

Hughes made his first start since the defeat at Villa, Roberts was suspended and Johnson was injured, whilst Fulham's injury list, which was dreadful in January, had much improved. After a scrappy opening, Albion had the chance to get into the lead in the fourth minute, when a great long ball sent Hughes away, but all he could manage was a weakish volley straight at the keeper.

Five minutes later, after McInnes had involuntarily blocked a shot from Melville in his own box, Albion broke away, and when Dichio nodded down, it was McInnes who had a pot-shot, from 25 yards, which went just over. Then it was Fulham's turn again; they broke down the right, Gregan got in a terrible mess, and Sava just failed to connect after a scramble. It really was end to end stuff, and immediately there was a similar scramble in the Fulham box, following two Koumas corners which the home side were lucky to clear.

Koumas was having a great game, and he really showed his skill in the 19th minute, with a sensational run. He beat four defenders after cutting in from the right, before pulling his shot a foot or two wide from fifteen yards. Fulham's best chance of the first half came in the 35th minute, when Malbranque and Sava broke clear, two on one; poor Gilchrist was tied up in knots, but the move ended with Malbranque shooting over from fifteen yards.

Three minutes before the break, both sides could have scored. First Hoult was all at sea with a cross from the right, which ended with Sava's flicked being cleared off the line magnificently by Gilchrist. From the goal kick which followed after the corner had been wasted, Jason Koumas broke down the right and crossed low for Hughes, in acres of space, on the left. He ran in, unmarked, shuffled his feet – and shot straight at Taylor. It was probably his worst-ever miss in his two spells at the club...

Albion had the first half chance of the second half, in the 51st minute, when Hughes beat the offside trap for once, and sprinted into the area. He lifted the ball over Ouaddou, only to get flattened, in the area; it was no penalty, but was definitely obstruction, but Rennie gave nothing.

Hoult then saved from Malbranque's volley – had it gone a foot either side of where it did, then the keeper would have had no chance; the same player, who was red hot all game, shot just wide, as Fulham stepped up the pressure once again, leading to a clearance a yard off the line by Moore after another Clement mix-up.

For all the brief pressure, there was still nothing between the teams, so it was quite a shock when Albion collapsed. Poor old Dobie – he came on just before the deluge, and didn't touch the ball for ten minutes.

It all went wrong in the 71st minute, when the ball was swung in from deep on the left, and there was no substantial challenge, allowing **SAHA** to dive in and bravely beat Hoult to the ball. Immediately Koumas went on another fantastic 40 yard run, beating five men, only to see Maik Taylor pull off a fine low save.

In the 73rd minute Gregan needlessly took out Marlet; from the free kick, 30 yards out, the ball was touched to **WOME**, who fired in a stunning drive which beat Hoult all ends up as it sped into the top corner. It was his first goal in English football.

In the 75th minute Inamoto broke down the left, and sent over a worrying cross; not so worrying, though, that Clement had to do his Corporal Jones impression, panic, and push Saha in the back. **MALBRANQUE** continued his excellent recent scoring run by scoring from the penalty. Three goals in five minutes – it was frightening!

*Attendance: 27,042*
*Referee: Mike Dean (The Wirral)*
*Assistants: S Proctor-Green & S Gagen*

# ALBION 1            WEST HAM U. 2
*Dichio 51*                    *Sinclair 45+1, 67*

| Russell HOULT | 01-01 | David JAMES |
|---|---|---|
| Adam CHAMBERS | 22-02 | Thomas REPKA |
| Ifeanyi UDEZE | 24-05 | Lee BOWYER [85] |
| Derek McINNES [74] | 04-06 | Michael CARRICK |
| Darren MOORE | 05-08 | Trevor SINCLAIR |
| Phil GILCHRIST | 06-19 | Ian PEARCE |
| Jason KOUMAS | 18-11 | Steve LOMAS |
| Lee HUGHES | 19-23 | Glen JOHNSON |
| Sean GREGAN | 14-10 | Paolo DI CANIO [49] |
| Daniel DICHIO | 09-22 | Les FERDINAND [81] |
| Ronnie WALLWORK [74] | 07-24 | Rufus BREVETT |
| Scott DOBIE [74] | 12-15 | Gary BREEN [85] |
| Larus SIGURDSSON [74] | 17-09 | Jermain DEFOE [49] |
| Des LYTTLE | 25-04 | Don HUTCHINSON [81] |
| Neil CLEMENT | 03-16 | John MONCUR |
| Joe MURPHY | 31-17 | Rai VAN DER GOUW |

## THE MATCH IN BRIEF
Albion throw away their best chance of survival in an incredible
match against West Ham, missing four gilt-edged chances as the
Hammers leapfrog them in the table.

## THE BUILD-UP

*Thursday February 20* It looks as if lee Hughes will get the nod once again ahead of Scott Dobie, for the visit of West Ham on Sunday; the most important game of the season so far.

*Saturday:* Results go Albion way, with Sunderland beaten at home by Middlesbrough, and Bolton held at home by Manchester United.:

## THE GAME

When the history of this season is written this will probably be the game that finally 'sent them down.' Of course, it's never over until the fat lady sings, but certainly the orchestra is warming up, and the diva is already doing her gargling... There was one change in the Albion side from the game at Fulham, Clement, as expected, being dropped in favour of Udeze. West Ham were without Kanoute and Cole.

It was Albion that went closest first, in the seventh minute. Jason Koumas was fouled wide on the left; he took the free kick himself, and placed the ball on the head of Darren Moore, who slammed a header against the far post, the ball being cleared from the rebound before Hughes could get to it. Ten minutes later, from a similar position, Les Ferdinand sent his far post header over the bar.

There was a good spell from Albion then, with Jason Koumas curling a free kick, for a foul on Dichio, on the edge of the box, over the bar. In the 25th minute, they actually got the ball into the net, thanks to a great one-two between Dichio and Udeze, which saw the latter neatly slip the ball under James. Unfortunately , the assistant referee gave offside against Udeze, who was certainly not, whilst Hughesie was hovering in a near-offside, but irrelevant position. Cruel luck.

In the 37th minute Russell Hoult horribly spilled Carrick's shot, right to the inrushing Trevor Sinclair. It was as bad an error as Kolinko's, which sent us up last season, but this time Sinclair went for the drive into the ground which, miraculously, bounced up and hit the bar.

In the first few moments of injury time in the first half, Steve Lomas clipped in a totally innocuous cross, which **SINCLAIR** brought down, crossed Moore, and slammed a shot across Hoult into the far corner. There was barely enough time to restart the game; what a stunner...

It took Albion just six minutes to get back on level terms. Udeze won a corner on the left, taken by Koumas; when Ferdinand headed clear, Koumas got the ball back and clipped it in for **DICHIO** to score with a great header. It was all back up for grabs. Two minutes later, Dichio was there again to nod down for Hughes, only for James to make a fantastic reflex save from his hook shot. Then, in the 57th minute, they had the ball into the net again, but this time Dichio was offside as he slid in Hughes' cross.

In the 58th minute Brevett flattened Chambers in the box; it was only just inside the area, but the referee decided it was outside, and Koumas' free kick was nowhere near as effective as the penalty Albion deserved.

In the 67th minute, West Ham, having soaked up all the pressure, took the lead again, this time thanks to another Hoult error. It was his poor kick out that allowed Lee Bowyer to hook in a cross from the right; substitute Defoe cushioned the ball back in from the far post for Ferdinand to head against the crossbar, only for **SINCLAIR** to head the rebound past Hoult and Gilchrist on the line.

Cue some awful misses; in the 70th minute Hughes brilliantly anticipated a bad headed back pass from Sinclair, only for James to make fantastic save from his toe-poke. Four minutes later, on came Scott Dobie, and his first touch saw him race clear of three vacillating defenders, onto a Dichio head on. He had just James to beat, but the much maligned keeper spread himself well to block – even so, it was a bad miss. There was still time for one more one-on-one miss; ten minutes from time another Dichio header put Hughes away, and once again, he was unable to beat James from close range.

*Attendance: 31,915*
*Referee: Dermot Gallagher (Banbury)*
*Assistants: G Beale & R Bone*

# SOUTHAMPTON 1    ALBION 0

*Beattie 7*

| | | |
|---|:---:|---|
| Antti NIEMI | 14-01 | Russell HOULT |
| Claus LUNDEKVAM | 05-17 | Larus SIGURDSSON |
| Wayne BRIDGE | 03-24 | Ifeanyi UDEZE [25] |
| Michael SVENSSON | 11-04 | Derek McINNES [76] |
| Matt OAKLEY | 08-05 | Darren MOORE |
| Paul TELFER | 33-06 | Phil GILCHRIST |
| Chris MARSDEN | 04-14 | Sean GREGAN |
| Anders SVENSSON [28] | 12-19 | Lee HUGHES |
| James BEATTIE | 09-09 | Daniel DICHIO |
| Fabrice FERNADES [90] | 29-07 | Ronnie WALLWORK[HT] |
| Brett ORMEROD [76] | 36-18 | Jason KOUMAS |
| David PRUTTON [28] | 20-03 | Neil CLEMENT [25] |
| Jo TESSEM [76] | 21-20 | JORDAO [76] |
| Danny HIGGINBOTHAM [90] | 19-12 | Scott DOBIE [HT] |
| Jason DODD | 02-23 | Adam CHAMBERS |
| Paul JONES | 01-31 | Joe MURPHY |

**THE MATCH IN BRIEF**
More controversy, as the Albion claim that the ball ran out of play
in the move that saw the only goal of the game, from hot-shot
James Beattie, in the seventh minute.

## THE BUILD-UP

*Wednesday February 26* Gary Megson has a go at somebody or other. "There were one or two people on the periphery of things who were pleased with Sunday's result because they felt it served their own cause. Those dissenting voices will not be allowed to disturb the fantastic spirit at this club." Paul Thompson was believed to be the target.

*Friday*: Now Megson denies that there is a rift between him and Testimonial man Bob Taylor...

## THE GAME

It was a gala day for Albion fans, in that it was a new ground; indeed, it was the club's first visit to Southampton for seventeen years. The Saints had only lost two games at their St Mary's Stadium all season – the last two, in fact, against United and Liverpool – and it was clear this would be a toughie. In fact, Albion did not even bother to compete in the first half, and whilst it can be said that they were unjustly treated, should have had two penalties, and the winner should not have been allowed, it has to be conceded that they were simply not good enough.

In the second minute McInnes sent Lee Hughes away, but, lacking in confidence, he shot too early, just past the post from 25 yards. Four minutes later Moore gave away a corner, and when Russell Hoult was beaten at the near post, the header flashed inches wide, Beattie getting to it just too late, and heading into the side-netting.

He was more accurate sixty seconds later, albeit controversially. Telfer took the ball down the right, but appeared to have run the ball out of play. The Albion players all appealed, and let him get on with it, and when he exchanged passes and lobbed in a cross, it dropped for **BEATTIE**, who smashed a tremendous drive past a static Hoult from all over 30 yards – next month's Goal of The Month on the Premiership, and his 19th goal of the season. Cue a lot of moaning, to no avail, to referee Dermot Gallagher.

The Saints turned the screw; Marsden nearly crept in at the far post, Fernandes – the real playmaker in the side – had a shot blocked and then, in the 23rd minute, big Norwegian Lundekvam missed an open goal. Seven minutes later, Ormerod nearly had the same freedom of movement, only a good late challenge from Siggy putting him off, six yards out. Five minutes before the break, Hoult made his first proper save, tipping Oakley's 30 yarder round the post – only for the referee and linesman to miss his touch, and give a goal kick. It was about the only break Albion got...

Right on the half time whistle, Hoult was in action again, tipping over another superb volley from Ormerod.

Post-dressing down, with Dobie on for Wallwork, Albion were better, although within two minutes Ormerod had the ball in the net, only to see the goal disallowed for a foul by Beattie. Three minutes later, Hoult tipped Fernandes' shot against the bar, and over, but that was a last hurrah for Saints. Albion began to take over, without actually hitting any heights. In the 72nd minute Lee Hughes was hauled down in the box, without reward, and so slack was the Saints' defence at times that an enraged Strachan actually ran ten yards onto the pitch to remonstrate with them during play!

Ten minutes from time, a Saints defender appeared to handle in the box to prevent Sigurdsson's winning a header, but was not spotted, and then Koumas went on a great sixty yard run, only to see his shot blocked. The closest Albion came to a goal was in the 88th minute, when Hughes dug out a simple sidefoot at goal that was deflected by Dichio onto the post, and out, from six yards range, and then again, in the third minute of injury time, when Albion were throwing everybody up, and Dichio had a good chance blocked at close range. Too little, too late – although the Albion fans were singing a new song at the end, "The Premier League is fixed."

*Attendance: 27,024*
*Referee: Andy D'Urso (Billericay)*
*Assistants: S Proctor-Green & T Massey*

# ALBION 0     CHELSEA 2

*Stanic 37, Zola 55*

| | | |
|---|---|---|
| Russell HOULT | 01-23 | Carlo CUDICINI |
| Igor BALIS | 02-15 | Mario MELCHIOT |
| Ifeanyi UDEZE [HT] | 24-26 | John TERRY |
| Derek McINNES [16] | 04-13 | William GALLAS |
| Darren MOORE [16] | 05-12 | Mario STANIC [73] |
| Sean GREGAN | 14-08 | Frank LAMPARD |
| Jason KOUMAS | 18-20 | Jody MORRIS |
| Lee HUGHES | 19-14 | Graham LE SAUX [82] |
| Jason ROBERTS | 11-25 | Gianfranco ZOLA |
| Larus SIGURDSSON | 17-09 | Jimmy HASSELBAINK |
| Jason KOUMAS | 18-22 | Eidur GUDJOHNSEN[55] |
| Scott DOBIE | 12-06 | Marcel DESAILLY [82] |
| James CHAMBERS [16] | 22-21 | Enrique DE LUCAS [73] |
| Daniel DICHIO [HT] | 09-30 | Jesper GRONKJAER [55] |
| Ronnie WALLWORK [16] | 07-39 | Carlton COLE |
| Joe MURPHY | 31-01 | Ed DE GOEY |

**THE MATCH IN BRIEF**
Not only do Albion lose — comprehensively — to a classy Chelsea side at The Hawthorns; they also lose Darren Moore to injury for the rest of the season

### THE BUILD-UP

*Wednesday March 12* Gary Megson is now being linked with the Leeds job, which, as rumour has it, will soon become available.

### THE GAME

In a mind-numbingly dull game against Chelsea, Albion virtually surrendered their Premiership place without a fight. Indeed, it took them 76 minutes to get a shot on target. Yet after just 40 seconds, Jason Roberts, back after three games' suspension, sent Balis – also back after a long spell out – away on the overlap, and when he crossed low, Hughes miskicked and Roberts, off-balance, volleyed the ball wide. Six minutes later, Udeze cut out a short crossfield pass from Jody Morris, but his far post cross was just too far. So far, not too bard, with Albion on top, but in the 16th minute the team suffered a double blow when they lost first Darren Moore, then Derek McInnes.

Moore collided heavily with Hasselbaink and put a lot of weight onto a twisted knee. As he was being stretchered off, Derek McInnes also limped off the pitch, with Wallwork and Chambers coming on. It didn't cost Albion the game, but it didn't help, either... In the 24th minute, in their first decent attack, Chelsea should have gone ahead. A poor Sigurdsson challenge was brushed off by Jimmy Floyd Hasselbaink, and he took on two more defenders in a forty yard run that ended with a superb blocking save by Hoult, who pushed the ball away for a corner.

At this point, Chelsea were showing all the ball skill, keeping possession just as readily as Albion were prepared to squander it, but, otherwise, there wasn't a huge gulf between the sides. However, in the 37th minute, there was a goal between them, scored by the Londoners. Zola – who should be the Player of the Year this season – won a corner on the Chelsea right, curled it in himself and Mario **STANIC** headed home from close range. Game over.

At the break, Udeze – called into the Nigerian squad at the weekend – was off, and Dichio was on, as Megson decided to go for broke, several weeks too late. he had an immediate effect, but lost his bearings, just inside the box, and headed a Roberts knock-down away from goal. Albion had several shots charged down, without really worrying anybody, before Hasselbaink broke away once more, in the 50th minute, and it took another brave blocking save from Hoult to stop the Dutchman. Five minutes later, and it was 2-0. Haselbaink, of course, was involved, playing a lovely one-two with **ZOLA**, who made a bit of room before drilling a great low shot just inside Hoult's left hand post.

On 69 minutes Chelsea fashioned a beautiful moved that ended with Zola setting up Hasselbaink to drive inches past the post. In the sunshine, Albion fans were too busy dreaming of visits to Crewe and Grimsby next season...

Then Jason Koumas – our best performer by a mile – had a flurry of shots on goal, almost all of them scurrying past the post. One of them, though, was on target – a measured curler that had Cudicini flinging himself, in typical Continental style, to make the save look harder than it was. Sixty seconds later the SuperBob chants started, which must have pleased Bob, who was sitting in the stands. The closest Albion came to a goal was in the 85th minute, when a Chelsea defender forced Cudicini to another grand save, thus preventing a spectacular own goal.

*Darren Moore — out for the rest of the season*

*Attendance: 29,449*
*Referee: Paul Durkin (Dorset)*
*Assistants: D Bryan & D Morrison*

# BIRMINGHAM C. 1  ALBION 0

*Horsfield 90+4*

| | | |
|---|---|---|
| Ian BENNETT | 01-01 | Russell HOULT |
| Jeff KENNA [66] | 02-02 | Igor BALIS |
| Kenny CUNNINGHAM | 12-03 | Neil CLEMENT |
| Jamie CLAPHAM | 23-04 | Derek McINNES |
| Matthew UPSON | 25-24 | Ifeanyi UDEZE |
| Stephen CLEMENCE[77] | 32-17 | Larus SIGURDSSON |
| Paul DEVLIN | 07-14 | Sean GREGAN |
| Robbie SAVAGE | 08-19 | Lee HUGHES |
| Clinton MORRISON [55] | 19-09 | Daniel DICHIO |
| Christophe DUGARRY | 21-07 | Ronnie WALLWORK |
| Damien JOHNSON | 22-18 | Jason KOUMAS [85] |
| Stern JOHN [77] | 14-19 | Lee HUGHES [85] |
| Darren CARTER [66] | 24-25 | Des LYTTLE |
| Geoff HORSFIELD [55] | 09-12 | Scott DOBIE |
| Michael JOHNSON | 17-22 | James CHAMBERS |
| Andy MARRIOTT | 36-31 | Joe MURPHY |

**THE MATCH IN BRIEF**
Four minutes into injury time Albion lose a game that almost certainly condemns them to the First Division; yet a draw was the least that they deserved on the balance of play

## THE BUILD-UP

*Monday March 17* Darren Moore's season is now over; the tough defender will be out for around sixth months after suffering cruciate ligament damage against Chelsea yesterday.

*Wednesday*: It's also looking grim for Michael Appleton's career. The former Manchester United midfielder goes into hospital for a third operation on his injured knee, after failing to make the first team in his latest comeback.

*Friday*: Some good news at last; it looks as if Derek McInnes, who limped off at the same time as Moore, will make the big West Midlands Derby game which kicks off at noon on Saturday.

## THE GAME

Manager Gary Megson came in for some heavy criticism – possibly the worst in his entire stay at the Albion – after this dreadful defeat at St Andrews. Yet the performance, overall, was one of the most solid of the season. Albion were, on the whole, pretty much in control. But if you can't score goals, the best you'll ever get is a nil-nil – and that simply wouldn't have been good enough on the day.

The game kicked off at noon in glorious bright sunshine. The first half was pretty tedious. In the third minute, Clemence had plenty of space in front of goal, after a knock down, but blazed over the bar. Then a Johnson cross spun off Wallwork, ten yards out; it could have gone anywhere, but fortunately went straight to Hoult. The longer the game went on, the more confident Albion got. In the 23rd minute, Dichio hooked in a cross that reached Udeze – who had his best game so far – but the Nigerian sent a screamer just over the bar. Two minutes later Roberts twisted and turned in the box and beat Upson to the ball, only to be brought down from behind. It looked a sure penalty for anybody but us or Manchester City, but the referee just walked away...

Albion were now slightly on top, but they could have gone a goal down in the 38th minute, from the first move of quality, when Dugarry turned a long ball inside for Morrison, but, with the ball slightly behind him, the hated ex-Palace man shot wide.

The second half started with a good run by Koumas, which ended with a cross from Balis that Dichio could not reach. Three minutes later Koumas was in the thick of it again, playing a one-two with Roberts before firing in a good low shot that Bennett could not hold, the ball being hacked away for a corner.

From the corner, Albion got as close as they were going to get to a goal, when Gregan headed on for Roberts to flick a header against the crossbar from four yards. That was the distance that Dubarry was, sixty seconds later, when he got up to a free header which, fortunately, Hoult was able to parry brilliantly with his legs. It was getting quite exciting now, and just after Bennett only just managed to reach a first time stabbed lob by McInnes, from out on the left, after he had been put through by Gregan.

After 62 minutes Russell Hoult dropped a high cross under pressure from Dugarry, but when the Frenchman went for goal, Clement was there to clear off the line. In fact, it was all Dugarry at this point; he headed into Hoult's arms, then over the bar when well placed. In the 66th minute, Darren Carter should have won it, when Savage beat McInnes on the right and put over the perfect hanging cross, but the young substitute mistimed his header, right in front of goal, and put it wide.

As Blues pressed hungrily forward, a good run by Jamie Clapham was hooked out of Hoult's arms by Clement, then Hoult made a great fingertip save from substitute Horsfield's header. Five minutes from time – too little, too late – Megson brought on Hughes (fair enough) but took off his side's best player by far, to jeers from the Railway End. Right on time, Stern John put wide with another misdirected header, but four minutes later there was no such mistake. John was allowed to chest the ball down on the six yard box, and twist and turn to get in a shot. The ball spun up into the air, and there was **HORSFIELD** to head home at the far post. There was no time left to restart the game...

*Attendance: 30,187*
*Referee:  Mark Halsey (Lancashire)*
*Assistants: R Martin & N Miller*

# MIDDLESBROUGH 3    ALBION 0

*Christie 37, Greening 76, Nemeth 87*

| Marck SCHWARZER | 01-01 | Russell HOULT |
|---|---|---|
| Franck QUEDRUE | 03-02 | Igor BALIS [85] |
| Colin COOPER | 28-03 | Neil CLEMENT |
| DORIVA | 20-04 | Derek McINNES [59] |
| Ugo EHIOGU | 04-17 | Larus SIGURDSSON |
| Gareth SOUTHGATE | 06-06 | Phil GILCHRIST |
| GEREMI | 14-14 | Sean GREGAN |
| Joseph-Desire JOB [70] | 16-11 | Jason ROBERTS [54] |
| Malcolm CHRISTIE [70] | 19-09 | Daniel DICHIO |
| JUNINHO [90] | 10-07 | Ronnie WALLWOR |
| Jonathan GREENING | 12-18 | Jason KOUMAS |
| Szilard NEMETH [70] | 08-25 | Des LYTTLE [85] |
| Massimo MACCARONE[70] | 09-10 | Andy JOHNSON [59] |
| Robbie STOCKDALE[90] | 02-12 | Scott DOBIE [54] |
| Brad JONES | 35-19 | Lee HUGHES |
| Luke WILKSHIRE | 31-31 | Joe MURPHY |

**THE MATCH IN BRIEF**
This display had the hallmark of a side that knew it was down;
Albion were dreadful and could have conceded seven or eight goals
against a Middlesbrough side who could not shoot straight

### THE BUILD-UP

*Wednesday April 2:* Chairman Jeremy Peace announces that he is considering buying Paul Thompson's 29% shareholding, triggering a takeover bid for the club.

*Friday:* After a Reserve game in the week, it looks as if Phil Gilchrist will start the game at Middlesbrough on Saturday.

### THE GAME

In the fifth minute Malcolm Christie cut in from the right wing to present a perfect chance for Job, and it took a marvellous save from Hoult to stop a fierce ten yarder. Sixty seconds later, Christie was in acres of space out on the wing again. This time he decided to take the responsibility himself, coming inside, cutting across the area, only to top his shot from just inside the box, giving Hoult an easy stop.

In the 21st minute Neil Clement sent Roberts away on the left, and he cut in, beat two defenders, then lashed his shot into the near post, where Schwarzer – coincidentally, another player who once turned us down in favour of 'Boro – just managed to push the ball away for a corner.

From the corner Sigurdsson lifted the ball over the bar from five yards, with the home defence in a real mess. Soon after Boro' broke splendidly down the right through Geremi, and when he put over the perfect cross Christie made a terrible hash of it right in front of goal. Minutes later Albion were cut wide open down the same flank, and this time two shots were blocked by defenders' bodies before Greening

pulled his shot wide from 15 yards.

The worst miss so far came in the 33rd minute, when Greening crossed for Job, just twelve yards out, but somehow he snatched at the shot and missed. The opening goal came in the 37th minute, when **CHRISTIE** cut in from the left, went through two feeble challenges, then sent a reverse-shot to Hoult's right, wrongfooting everybody.

Could the second half be as one-sided? Yes. Three minutes in Hoult spilled a Geremi shot straight to Job, then made amends by getting a touch to the follow-up, six yards out, and deflecting it outside. Then Christie set up a golden chance for Job, ten yards out, to pick his spot, but he shot wide again.

Juninho and Geremi both had shots saved by Hoult, then Boro' took off the worst culprits in front of goal, Job and Christie, and reaped the benefits. In the 76th minute **GREENING** took a one-two in his stride and slipped the ball under Hoult for the second goal. Then, amazingly, Albion should have broken their near-400 minute goal drought, when Balis put over a perfect cross, for the unmarked Dichio to head wide from ten yards.

In the 85th minute Des Lyttle came on for his first Premiership action since he left Forest, replacing Balis. Two minutes later another Slovakian, **NEMETH**, wrapped things up when he took a pass in his stride, went past Wallwork as if he wasn't there, and clipped the ball over the advancing Hoult.

*Slovakian international Szilard Nemeth scores the third goal at the Riverside Stadium*

*Attendance: 27,039*
*Referee: Steve Bennett (Kent)*
*Assistants: B Baker & C Bassindale*

# ALBION 1      EVERTON 2

*Balis 18 pen*       *Hoult (og) 23, Campbell 45*

| | | |
|---|---|---|
| Russell HOULT | 01-01 | Richard WRIGHT |
| Igor BALIS | 02-02 | Steve WATSON [81] |
| Neil CLEMENT [81] | 03-04 | Alan STUBBS |
| Derek McINNES [78] | 04-05 | David WEIR |
| Ronnie WALLWORK | 07-06 | David UNSWORTH |
| Sean GREGAN | 14-11 | Mark PEMBRIDGE [71] |
| Larus SIGURDSSON | 17-09 | Kevin CAMPBELL |
| Lee HUGHES | 19-16 | Thomas GRAVESEN [76] |
| Andy JOHNSON | 10-18 | Joseph YOBO |
| Daniel DICHIO | 09-20 | Wayne ROONEY |
| Jason KOUMAS | 18-26 | Lee CARSLEY |
| Scott DOBIE [78] | 12-10 | Duncan FERGUSON [81] |
| James CHAMBERS | 22-15 | Gary NAYSMITH [71] |
| Ifeanyi UDEZE [81] | 09-17 | Scot GEMMILL [76] |
| Des LYTTLE | 25-12 | Li TIE |
| Joe MURPHY | 31-35 | Paul GERRARD |

### THE MATCH IN BRIEF
Even after the benefit of a dubious penalty — their first of the season — Albion let it slip against a very average Everton side, Wayne Rooney and all. There is, however, a stay of execution...

## THE BUILD-UP

*Thursday:* More bad news for the Albion boss, as Phil Gilchrist is ruled out of the team for the rest of the season, with knee ligament problems.

*Friday:* And Gary Megson's future at the club is still not settled. He has still to sign a new contract; "I'll sit down with the chairman at the end of the season and sort that one out."

## THE GAME

It was not until the 12th minute that Champions League-chasing Everton began to show, and, inevitably, it was their new sensation, Wayne Rooney, who was at the thick of it, skipping through both Wallwork and Siggy to stab the ball wide from fifteen yards. A lovely Albion move then saw Balis set up Koumas to send in a fine half volley straight 'down the throat' of the keeper, and the same player – once again, Albion's best player by some way – went close soon after. Albion were now playing well, with enthusiasm and no little skill, but the manner in which they got their breakthrough was totally unexpected – a penalty!

Albion's first spot kick of the season – remarkably, exactly twelve months on from the last one, at Bradford last season – came when Stubbs accidentally handled a long ball in the box, under pressure from Dichio. It was harsh, and ultimately, got the Everton boss banished to the old directors' box for arguing about it. **BALIS** was given the ball and the Slovakian sent the keeper the wrong way, with 18 minutes gone.

The lead was held for five minutes; Rooney won a corner, and, under pressure from Weir, **HOULT** punched Pembridge's kick into the net. Everton were resurgent, and two minutes later Yobo scored with a great diving header at the far post, only to be given offside.

Then came the fightback from the Baggies. First Dichio headed on for Hughes to shoot straight at the keeper from sixteen yards. Then Balis put in Hughes again, and after beating two in the box, he shot across goal, but, somehow, Andy Johnson failed to put the ball over the line from a foot out.

Still, they usually go over the bar, anyway...

In the 37th minute, Wallwork was at fault, letting in Rooney, and it took a great double save from Hoult to stop the England man. Back to the other end, it what was fast becoming a real thriller, and the Balis-Hughes combination worked its magic again, but this time it was Ronnie Wallwork who was unable to score from a yard, admittedly from a very fast cross.

On 44 minutes, Everton really should have scored again, when Weir had a free header from another tricky inswinging Pembridge corner, but he sent his header wide. No mind; sixty seconds later, just as the game was going into injury time, Everton did take an undeserved lead. In came the cross from the right, Hoult flapped at it, and the ball dropped, right on the bye-line, for Rooney, who picked up another 'assist' by coolly tapping the ball across for **CAMPBELL** to roll the ball home from three yards.

The second half was nowhere near as good, as it faded away, and things got quite nasty – not helped by the fact that Gregan and Sigurdsson were clearly out to get Rooney, whilst Pembridge had twice elbowed Balis in the face and got away with it. The undercurrent was always there, and it did not help the game.

Inevitably, Rooney stood out. In the 59th minute he took advantage of another Sigurdsson error to run in on goal, but shot into the side-netting. Then, ten minutes later, Pembridge put him away, one on one on Gregan, and he outpaced the Albion man to force a great save from Hoult at the near post. Albion's one clear chance of the second half fell to Dichio, when Balis put over the perfect cross. Ten yards out, Dichio tried a convoluted scissors kick when a blasted shot would have been better, and put the ball wide.

Elsewhere, Blues beat Sunderland, and relegated them. Bolton lost at Chelsea, which earned the second biggest cheer of the day, after the penalty, which meant that Albion had one more match left as a top flight side...

*Attendance: 36,025*
*Referee: Graham Poll (Herts)*
*Assistants: D Morrison & A Woolmer*

# SUNDERLAND 1    ALBION 2

*Stewart 70*                    *McInnes 39, 42*

| Sunderland | | Albion |
|---|---|---|
| Mart POOM | 40-01 | Russell HOULT |
| Michael GRAY | 03-02 | Igor BALIS |
| Gavin McCANN [19] | 08-03 | Neil CLEMENT |
| Darren WILLIAMS | 18-04 | Derek McINNES |
| Jody CRADDOCK | 17-07 | Ronnie WALLWORK |
| Talal EL KARKOURI [58] | 22-14 | Sean GREGAN |
| Kevin KYLE [83] | 19-17 | Larus SIGURDSSON |
| Sean THORNTON | 24-19 | Lee HUGHES [36] |
| Kevin PHILLIPS | 10-10 | Andy JOHNSON |
| Marcus STEWART | 31-09 | Daniel DICHIO |
| Kevin KILBANE | 11-18 | Jason KOUMAS |
| Julio ARCA [19] | 33-12 | Scott DOBIE |
| George McCARTNEY [58] | 27-11 | Jason ROBERTS [36] |
| Michael PROCTOR [83] | 32-24 | Ifeanyi UDEZE |
| Tore Andre FLO | 09-25 | Des LYTTLE |
| Thomas SORENSEN | 01-31 | Joe MURPHY |

**THE MATCH IN BRIEF**
The team that lost at The Stadium of Light would almost certainly finish bottom, with the record of the worst side ever to play in the Premiership; Albion just about edge the game

### THE BUILD-UP

*Friday*: Tomorrow's game with Sunderland is the Relegation Cup Final, to decide which team will go in the record books as the worst-ever Premiership side.

### THE GAME

In the fifth minute a bad error by Wallwork let in Kevin Kyle, who cut in from the left to fire in a good low shot that Hoult saved at the foot of the post. A minute later, Kevin Kilbane went on a stunning ninety yard run which cut through the Albion defence like the proverbial hot knife, and he was unlucky when his shot spun up off Sigurdsson, and over the bar.

The corner was almost productive; it was flicked on by a near post header, to the far post, where Marcus Stewart was unmarked. He headed back, only for Hoult to make a brilliant save. The ball was cleared, put back in again from the same side, and this time Stewart headed against the post, with Hoult well-beaten.

How things changed with the introduction of Jason Roberts. Within three minutes Albion were ahead, with their first shot on target. Clement put the ball in from the left and Dichio went up for it with Poom, but, as usual, he was beaten to the ball by his marker. Unfortunately for Sunderland, Talal El Karkouri also got his goalkeeper as well; Poom dropped the ball like a hot potato, as his own man crashed into him, and of all people, Derek **McINNES** was there first to cleverly dink the ball over a defender.

After more than a year without a goal, the Scot then hit two in four minutes. In the 42nd minute Dichio was fouled, 25 yards out, right in the centre of goal. Koumas curled in a measured shot, which had Poom going the wrong way, but he managed to get a foot to the ball, and as it fell on the line, **McINNES** threw himself at it to force it over the line.

Sunderland almost drew blood at the start of the second half when Gregan's mis-kick let in Marcus Stewart, Hoult saving well at the foot of the post. Then it was Jason Roberts' turn. For a while, he was untouchable, and El Karkouri, McCartney – his first touch after coming on as substitute for Karkouri – and Williams were booked, in the space of six minutes, all for fouls on Roberts. Albion's domination, which had lasted for all of 33 minutes, disappeared twenty minutes from time, when Thornton tried an optimistic long range shot that Hoult spilled horribly, allowing poacher **STEWART** the chance to lift the ball over him, just like McInnes' first goal.

Then it was backs to the wall – or, at least, as far back as they needed to go to defend against the poorest attack in the top flight. But there was an inevitability to it all; Sunderland were awful, and they deserve to finish bottom. With Bolton beating West Ham, Albion's drop was also confirmed.

*Derek McInnes takes advantage of a defensive collision to beat Mart Poom for the first goal*

*Attendance: 26,899*
*Referee:  Phil Dowd (Stoke-on-Trent)*
*Assistants: N Bannister & S Gagen*

# ALBION 2      TOTTENHAM H. 3

*Dichio 24, Clement 61*     *Keane 45, 85, Sheringham 65*

| | | |
|---|---|---|
| Russell HOULT | 01-13 | Kasey KELLER |
| Igor BALIS | 02-02 | Stephen CARR |
| Ifeanyi UDEZE [57] | 24-05 | Goran BUNJEVCEVIC |
| Derek McINNES | 04-26 | Ledley KING |
| Ronnie WALLWORK | 07-30 | Anthony GARDNER |
| Sean GREGAN | 14-36 | Dean RICHARDS [82] |
| Larus SIGURDSSON | 17-29 | Simon DAVIES |
| Jason ROBERTS | 11-28 | Matthew ETHERINGTON |
| Andy JOHNSON | 10-44 | Kazuyuki TODA [HT] |
| Daniel DICHIO [69] | 09-10 | Teddy SHERINGHAM |
| Jason KOUMAS | 18-22 | Robbie KEANE |
| Scott DOBIE [69] | 12-14 | Gustavo POYET [HT] |
| James CHAMBERS | 22-06 | Chris PERRY [82] |
| Neil CLEMENT [57] | 24-21 | Milenko ACIMOVIC |
| Des LYTTLE | 25-16 | Steffen IVERSEN |
| Joe MURPHY | 31-01 | Neil SULLIVAN |

**THE MATCH IN BRIEF**
For the second successive game, normally shot-shy Albion score
twice, but this time it's not enough against a Tottenham side that is
chasing a UEFA Cup place

## THE BUILD-UP

*Saturday*: Paul Thompson is in danger of being ticked off by the Takeovers Panel, after his comments about Albion shares — "Worthless!" — following his recent sale of £2m worth of them to chairman Jeremy Peace.

## THE GAME

In the 11th minute Roberts left Gardner for dead on the bye line on the left, but his cut-back was just behind Dichio. Five minutes later Sigurdsson was lucky to get away with a slack pass, which left Keane in a two-on-two situation, but eventually the Iceman succeeded in winning the ball back. In the 19th minute Keane tried an overhead kick that had Hoult in trouble at the foot of the post; he spilled it, but when the Spurs man collected and shot at goal, the referee inexplicably awarded a goal kick.

By now, Albion were in full flow, and they took the lead in the 24th minute. Roberts went on a run down the right, but lost the ball; as it squirmed out, Koumas cleverly went for an instant cross, to the far post, where **DICHIO**, with one man on him, did well to stretch and head past Keller at the far post.

Spurs should have been level by the 33rd minute when Keane, taking advantage of Udeze going walkabout again, laid the ball on a plate for Simon Davies, but his shot was well blocked by Sigurdsson. Two minutes later, and it was Albion's turn, when, in a great move, Johnson headed down Roberts' cross for Keller to make a scrambling save from a super McInnes volley.

In the 39th minute, the game looked won, when Clement cleared a corner to set Jason Roberts free on the halfway line. It was almost comical to see Jason race away, with Gardner on his back all the way, but unable to get in a tackle because he knew that a foul would mean a certain red card. Roberts went right through, netted, then turned round to find out that the referee had given a foul against him for tugging Gardner's shirt back on the halfway line!

Just as the fourth official's board went up to show two minutes added time, Tottenham struck with a goal of great simplicity. Another one-two, this time between Sheringham and **KEANE**, saw the later stab the ball under Hoult from six yards range.

Spurs should have taken the lead early in the second half, when Etherington (who has recently been checked over by Megson) split the defence with a great pass. When the ball was pulled back to Poyet, he side-footed wide with the whole goal to aim at.

In the 57th minute Clement replaced the truly clueless Udeze. With his second touch of the ball, four minutes later, he put Albion ahead once more. After Richards had been booked for dissent after fouling Roberts, **CLEMENT**, with the ball moved ten yards to a more manageable 25 yards, smacked in a fantastic shot that would be a contender for *Goal of The Season* even in a normal year.

It took Spurs four minutes to get back in it, with a laughable goal. McInnes fouled King on the edge of the box; he chipped it up for Keane, who juggled the ball before sending in a terrible miskicked volley that was going well wide — until Goran Bunjevcevic, unmarked, six yards out, intervened. he headed against Hoult's left hand post and the ball dropped perfectly for **SHERINGHAM** to collect what we would hope would be the last of so many goals he has scored against the Baggies.

Spurs had the better of it after that. Etherington shot into the side-netting when he should have done better, and Sean Gregan nearly headed a corner into his own goal, although it took a great saving tackle from Gardner, in the box, to stop Roberts scoring.

It also took a fine save from Hoult to stop Carr fifteen minutes from time, but the points went west in the 85th minute. Ledley King sent over a eighty yard pass for **KEANE**, who, as at the game at Spurs, was in between two Albion defenders, but he managed to bring the ball down before angling a fine shot into the corner, for his 13th goal of the season (three against the Baggies). That stopped the mocking from the Smethwick End...

*Attendance: 27,128*
*Referee: Dermott Gallagher (Banbury)*
*Assistants: N Bannister & S Gagen*

# ALBION 0     LIVERPOOL 6

*Owen 18, 49, 60, 66 Baros 47, 85*

| | | |
|---|---|---|
| Russell HOULT | 01-01 | Jerzy DUDEK |
| Igor BALIS | 02-23 | Jamie CARRAGHER |
| Neil CLEMENT | 03-04 | Sami HYPPIA |
| Derek McINNES | 04-30 | Djimi TRAORE |
| Ronnie WALLWORK [55] | 07-18 | John Arne RIISE [80] |
| Sean GREGAN [86] | 14-09 | El Hadji DIOUF [70] |
| Andy JOHNSON | 10-17 | Steven GERRARD |
| Jason ROBERTS | 11-16 | Dietmar HAMANN |
| Daniel DICHIO | 09-13 | Danny MURPHY [84] |
| Ifeanyi UDEZE [73] | 24-05 | Milan BAROS |
| Jason KOUMAS | 18-10 | Michael OWEN |
| Scott DOBIE | 12-21 | Salif DIAO [80] |
| James CHAMBERS [55] | 22-08 | Emile HESKEY [70] |
| Des LYTTLE [73] | 25-28 | Bruno CHEYROU [84] |
| JORDAO [86] | 20-07 | Vladimir SMICER |
| Joe MURPHY | 31-19 | Pegguay ARPHEXAD |

## THE MATCH IN BRIEF
Champions League-chasing Liverpool brush Albion aside, and inflicting on them their worst-ever home defeat in 115 years of League football. Michael Owen is the main destroyer, with four goals

### THE BUILD-UP

*Wednesday April 23*: Larus Sigurdsson will miss the Liverpool game because he has flown back to Iceland for the funeral of his grandmother.

### THE GAME

From the off, Liverpool's patient build-up spelled doom for the Baggies. They passed the ball around as if the Albion weren't there, and the surprise was that Liverpool only got one goal in the first half. That came in the 18th minute, when **OWEN** took a pass from Danny Murphy, fooled Clement with the speed of his spin off the ball, and outpaced the defender to strike a great shot across Hoult low into the corner.

Two minutes later, the unmarked Baros should have made it two, when he took a Murphy free kick eight yards out, but Hoult saved his low shot. Two minutes after that, after Murphy had had a long range effort blocked, Hamann sent in a glorious volley that beat Hoult, but whistled past the post. It was one way traffic now, and in the 24th minute came Baros' first bad miss; he was clean through, but dallied, allowing Gregan to get in enough of a challenge to put him off his shot, six yards out.

On the half hour mark, Albion were lucky again, when Owen ran onto a long ball and beat Gregan, only for Hoult to make a great save, gathering at the second attempt. Five minutes before the break, Albion actually fashioned a chance, but Dichio flashed his header wide from Koumas' well-placed corner. The last word of the half went, inevitably, to Owen, who forced Hoult to another wonderful save.

At the interval, Houllier told his team to be more ruthless – and it showed. Within two minutes following a Gerrard cross, **BAROS** put the ball over the line after a scramble in the box. Two minutes later, Udeze gifted a corner, and when that was badly cleared, Baros took the cross, and stumbled, but **OWEN** was in there as well, to put the ball over the line.

It was the England man's 100th Premiership goal for Liverpool.

Liverpool's fourth goal, on the hour mark, was ludicrous. Albion were attacking, and substitute James Chambers got in a shot; it was blocked, to Owen, and his pass sent Baros way down the right. With some subtle skills he bamboozled Clement and Gregan, and then rolled the ball over for **OWEN** to stroke home his hat-trick goal.

Six minutes later Owen became the first mean to score four at The Hawthorns since John Wark (also for Liverpool) two decades ago, Murphy slipping the ball through a static defence for **OWEN** to tuck it into the corner. Now it was 'shots in.' Hoult saved from Owen at the near post, Baros overran the ball after beating Clement and Gregan yet again, then Hamann put another effort over.

Nine minutes from time, Albion saw their first attacking action, when Koumas unleashed a great 25 yarder that Dudek saved spectacularly. It was a brief interlude; sixty seconds later Owen raced clean through again, looking for his fifth, but pulled his shot wide. The scoring was completed in the 85th minute; another simple long ball (which Albion had been trying all afternoon, without success) and **BAROS** was free to blast the ball under Hoult for 6-0.

In the 88th minute Owen missed another gilt-edged chance form Steven Gerrard's low cross, two yards out, and Hamann went close as well. How many Albion fans were even left in the ground to see the last bit of action at the Birmingham Road End? Balis placed the best cross of the match right on Dichio's head, six yards out – Dudek saved his diving header, and Robert's follow-up, which would have at least denied Liverpool their new record, was hacked away off — or from behind — the line by Hyppia. "This was an accident waiting to happen – it could have been double figures" admitted Gary Megson afterwards. As it was, it was Albion's record home defeat in 115 years of League football.

*Attendance: 27,470*
*Referee: Rob Styles (Hants)*
*Assistants: C Bassindale & J Devine*

# BLACKBURN R. 1      ALBION 1

*Duff 10*                               *Koumas 54*

| Brad FRIEDEL | 01-01 | Russell HOULT |
| Lucas NEILL | 02-22 | James CHAMBERS |
| TUGAY | 03-03 | Neil CLEMENT |
| Andy TODD | 04-04 | Derek McINNES |
| Garry FLITCROFT [66] | 07-07 | Ronnie WALLWORK |
| David DUNN | 08-25 | Des LYTTLE |
| Andy COLE | 09-14 | Sean GREGAN |
| Martin TAYLOR | 21-11 | Jason ROBERTS |
| Hakan SUKUR [60] | 33-09 | Daniel DICHIO [82] |
| Jay McEVELEY [70] | 34-10 | Andy JOHNSON |
| Damien DUFF | 11-18 | Jason KOUMAS |
| Nils-Eric JOHANSSON[70] | 14-02 | Igor BALIS |
| Craig HIGNETT [66] | 21-24 | Ifeanyi UDEZE |
| Dwight YORKE [60] | 19-12 | Scott DOBIE [82] |
| Egil OSTENSTAD | 22-19 | Lee HUGHES |
| Alan KELLY | 13-31 | Joe MURPHY |

**THE MATCH IN BRIEF**
On the day that Albion fans have their annual 'Away Day Party' —
this time the theme was 'The Men in Black' their team give a good
display to stymie Blackburn's UEFA Cup qualification hopes

### THE BUILD-UP

*Sunday April 27*: Jason Koumas is named as Albion's *Player of The Year*, with Gregan and Hoult second and third. Joe Murphy is Ireland's Under-21 *Player of The Year*.

### THE GAME

First blood went to the Albion, when Koumas tried a low shot from twenty yards. It had Friedel in some trouble, and he could only push the ball out at the post; Clement won possession, but his cross back in was not accurate enough.

Two minutes later, a grand sweeping move by the Albion, through Koumas, McInnes and Johnson ended with Clement crossing low again, and when Dichio missed the ball, Lyttle, coming in from behind, scuffed a shot well wide.

From a Rovers corner in the ninth minute, Gary Flitcroft found plenty of space, only to head the ball well over the bar. Soon after Andy Todd made a bit of room, but shot straight at Hoult. Not so Damien **DUFF**, in the tenth minute. He was found by a raking Lucas Neill pass, that bypassed Ronnie Wallwork to find the Irishman in acres of space on the Albion right, and he just took the ball on to just inside the box before lashing it across Hoult's diving body.

After that, Rovers looked comfortable, as they camped inside the Albion half. In a rare thrill, in the 19th minute, Dichio was first to a Wallwork cross, and sent a header into Friedel's hands. Two minutes later, Albion fluked a corner, because of a defensive miskick, and once again it was Dichio who bulleted a header from Koumas' flag-kick, which Friedel caught under his crossbar.

Albion came out fighting in the second half, and the longer it went on, the more obvious it became that Rovers were taking it easy, and just assuming that they would stroll to a victory and a UEFA Cup place for next season. It was never going to be that easy. In the 54th minute, out of the blue, Albion equalised. First Andy Johnson burst through the Rovers midfield. Jason **KOUMAS** took over, and made a marvellous run, beating two defenders over sixty yards, before lashing the ball high into the net – thanks to a deflection off Neill. One of the goals of the season, most people thought – although we're still sticking with Neil Clement's free kick.

Moments later, Albion should have won it. A long ball found Roberts in the clear, on the right hand side of the box, and he wriggled past Friedel, with the goal gaping, but delayed his shot – his confidence levels are so low now – allowing the American to dive down and push the ball away for a corner.

Albion gave at least as much as they got after that, and Rovers only started to look dangerous after Dwight Yorke replaced the ineffectual Sukur.

*Jason Koumas, left, beats Friedel with the help of a deflection off the flying boot of Neill*

*Attendance: 27,036*
*Referee: Graham Barber (Herts)*
*Assistants: K Stroud & N Miller*

## ALBION 2                    NEWCASTLE U. 2
*Dobie 57, 71*                *Jenas 45, Viana 80*

| | | |
|---|---|---|
| Russell HOULT | 01-01 | Shay GIVEN |
| James CHAMBERS [81] | 22-04 | Nolberto SOLANO [75] |
| Neil CLEMENT | 03-05 | Andrew O'BRIEN |
| Derek McINNES | 04-07 | Jermaine JENAS |
| Larus SIGURDSSON | 17-08 | Kieron DYER [89] |
| Ronnie WALLWORK | 07-12 | Andrew GRIFFIN |
| Jason KOUMAS | 18-18 | Aaron HUGHES [82] |
| Des LYTTLE | 25-20 | Lomana LUALUA |
| Bob TAYLOR [31] | 15-23 | Shola AMEOBI |
| Daniel DICHIO | 09-30 | Steven CALDWELL |
| Andy JOHNSON | 10-45 | Hugo VIANA |
| Igor BALIS | 02-28 | Michael CHOPRA [82] |
| Jason ROBERTS | 11-17 | Darren AMBROSE [75] |
| Scott DOBIE [31] | 12-19 | Titus BRAMBLE |
| Ifeanyi UDEZE [81] | 24-25 | Brian KERR [89] |
| Brian JENSEN | 31-13 | Stephen HARPER |

### THE MATCH IN BRIEF
The Baggies bow out of the Premiership with a creditable draw against a Newcastle side that had clinched their Champions League place a week earlier. Dobie's two goals give him a share of the top Albion League scorer spot

## THE BUILD-UP

*Friday May 9*: Jason Roberts declares that he would prefer to remain the Premiership next season. Spurs are reportedly interested.

*Saturday*: A big surprise, as Megson recalls Bob Taylor for his swansong, against Newcastle.

## THE GAME

In the fifth minute Taylor was flattened on the edge of the box, but Clement's free kick went tamely wide. Two minutes later Andy Johnson robbed Viana, and put in a quick cross that, a few years ago, Bob would have hit first time; this time he brought it down, but could not turn fast enough to get in a shot. In the 11th minute Newcastle got the ball in the net, but Ameobi, who had got in the end of Hughes' cross, was standing by himself on the goal line when he put it away, and for once the referee – who was doing the Cup Final the week after – gave offside.

In the 22nd minute, Albion should have scored, when a perfect McInnes chip put Andy Johnson through. Not the man you would want to put your mortgage on, and this time he lobbed the keeper, but the ball dropped on top of the net.

Tragedy struck for SuperBob in the 24th minute, when he fell awkwardly, and a stretcher was called for. He got to his feet, walked gingerly down the line, but it was clear he was in trouble. On the half hour mark he was given one last chance, when specifically instructed to get in the wall for a Clement free kick in the same position as the one against Crystal Palace last season. Could there be a repeat of that goal? No – because Clement's kick went sailing into the Newcastle fans at the Smethwick End. Immediately Bob limped off, to a standing ovation, to be replaced by Dobie. It was a sad ending to a great Albion career, particularly as the injury looked bad enough to threaten his place in his own Testimonial game, two days later.

Newcastle came more into it just before the interval. In the 43rd minute Sigurdsson was fortunate when he sliced a LuaLua cross, six yards out – neither he nor Hoult knew what was happening, as the ball just cleared his own bar. Two minutes later, Solano won a corner on the right, took it himself, and **JENAS**, criminally, was allowed to head in from almost on the line. In added time, it was almost two, but for a good Hoult save from LuaLua's near post drive.

Albion were under fire at the start of the second half as well, and it needed a touch from Andy Johnson to deflect Ameobi's header from a corner onto the underside of the bar, and out again. A few minutes later, Newcastle should have had a penalty when James Chambers handled in the area to stop Ameobi. Sixty seconds later the same Newcastle man went through and rounded Hoult, but this time Chambers stopped him legitimately, clearing his angled shot off the line right by the post.

A minute later, Albion got their first shot on target, when Dichio beat the offside trap after a one-two with Dobie, but his low shot on the turn, ten yards out, was well saved by Given. No matter; in the 57th minute, Albion equalised, when McInnes put over another accurate chip, and **DOBIE** ran onto it to poke the ball past Given.

Twice Hoult made good saves from LuaLua and Ameobi, as Newcastle fought back, but in the 71st minute Albion had a touch of luck, and went ahead. McInnes found Dobie, and he gave the ball to Clement who, in turn, supplied Koumas, and when his mediocre cross came in, the ball just dropped for **DOBIE** to sidefoot it first time just inside the post, the ball curling beyond Given.

In the 77th minute Viana had a scorching volley that, had it not gone straight to Hoult, would have been a super goal. Three minutes later we saw another example of the man's shooting ability, when Newcastle won a free kick just outside the box, and **VIANA** curled a corker inside the post, with Hoult well beaten. It was a deserved equaliser. The game, and the season, faded away from then on, as Newcastle contemplated Milan next season — and we looked up the route to Wigan.

# 2002-03 REVIEW

It had been a long time coming. Albion had suffered sixteen years in the wilderness before goals from Darren Moore and Bob Taylor, on the last day of the 2001-02 season, had returned the club back to the top flight. But things had changed significantly since Albion had last been there. The last time they were promoted, from old Division Two to One, in 1976, it was very unusual for clubs to come straight back down. Nowadays, in the Premiership, it is a rarity if at least one of the promoted clubs does not suffer an immediate drop back down to the Nationwide League. This time it was to be Albion's turn – the first time in their history that they had ever failed to consolidate after promotion.

The fixture computer certainly gave Albion fans the celebrate their entry to the Premiership, as the club opened its campaign at Old Trafford. A harsh sending off for captain Derek McInnes proved to be the start of some alarming refereeing decisions, as Albion went down to a single goal from Solskjaer. The gate of 67,645 was the biggest attendance, ever, for an Albion League game.

Seven days later, Albion gave another impressive display, at The Hawthorns, when they battered Terry Venables' Leeds side for the first forty minutes, only to ship three goals in quick succession as Leeds went top of the table. One of Megson's new signings, Lee Marshall, opened with a goal against Leeds; also in the side were defender Sean Gregan and – on the bench for the opening games — midfielder Ronnie Wallwork.

Then the ultimate test – Arsenal at Highbury when Albion were really found wanting. In a devastating first half, the Gunners destroyed the Albion defence, and although there were eventually goals for Roberts and Dobie, Arsenal could have won more easily than the final scoreline of 5-2.

There were two more new faces in the side to face Fulham at The Hawthorns. Straight back in the side went Lee Hughes, re-signed for a cut-price £2.5m after a year at Coventry, whilst coming off the bench was exciting Welsh midfielder Jason Koumas, recently bought from Tranmere after protracted negotiations that took almost a year to come to fruition.

Fulham provided Albion's first ever win in the Premiership, Darren Moore scoring the goal, and for a while, Albion's season took an upturn, as they recorded three wins in succession.

*Startling debut for Murphy*

Next victims were lowly West Ham, beaten by a Jason Roberts goal at Upton Park. Three days later it was Southampton's turn, although it took a late fluke goal from Sean Gregan to settle a game that had previously been dominated by the Saints. Albion were sitting pretty in the Premiership, in seventh place, three points above Manchester United. It would be eleven weeks before they would win again.

Their next two games were decided by contentious decisions. At Liverpool Russell Hoult became the first Albion goalkeeper to be sent off since Joe Reader a century before, when he brought down Michael Owen. Sensationally, new signing Joe Murphy – only on the bench because Brian Jensen had flu – saved Owen's spot kick with his first touch in an Albion shirt. However, after more than holding their own, and being denied a certain penalty, Albion's ten men succumbed to two goals form Baros and Riise.

In Albion's next game, they were dominating an ordinary-looking Blackburn Rovers side at The Hawthorns, until referee Halsey gave Rovers a penalty for a questionable offence that was clearly outside the box; another 2—0 defeat.

That was the first of two games in three days for Megson's men – but few of the side played in both games, as the manager practised 'squad rotation' for the Worthington Cup game at Wigan. There were rare outings for Des Lyttle and Jordao, and full debuts for Murphy and young full-back Lloyd Dyer. Albion crashed 3-1 to the Second Division pacesetters, but at least Lee Hughes scored his one – and only – goal of the season.

Another terrible pair of refereeing decisions cost Albion their next game, at St James' Park. First, Jason Roberts was hauled down by Andy O'Brien when clean through, but no red card was shown, and then, after Albion were well in control with an Igor Balis goal, the referee gifted them an equaliser when he decided that Balis had deliberately passed back to Murphy. The free kick, from ten yards, was smashed home by Alan Shearer, who went on to score the winner.

Of course, it was not just poor deci-

*Scott Dobie is within a whisker of giving the Albion the lead at Elland Road*

sions from the officials that was responsible for Albion's eventual relegation. In the home game with Birmingham City, Darren Moore scored what would be the first of three own goals scored by Albion defenders, some measure of the shakiness of the defence. It took an instant reply from Jason Roberts, in the dying moments of the game, to grab Albion a point That goal – Roberts' third in ten games – would be his last of the season, another reason why Albion would soon be struggling.

Chelsea – with Gianfranco Zola having an immaculate game – were too much for The Baggies at Stamford Bridge, and the side slipped back into the bottom three for the first time in two months. A defensive horror show allowed Manchester City to leave The Hawthorns with three points, but it was tactical naiveté that was responsible for the loss of two points at the Reebok the following week.

Early in the game Bolton were reduced to ten men by the sending off of Bruno Ngotty, and with Albion a goal up through Scott Dobie, a win looked a certainty. Inexplicably, Megson gave his team instructions to defend the penalty area for the rest of the game, and the home side scored a late equaliser.

For once, Albion had the better of the refereeing decisions in the home game with Aston Villa. Mr Gallagher gave the visitors one spot kick – brilliantly saved by Hoult – but missed another certain penalty. Even so, Albion had enough of the play to have got more than just a goalless draw.

On Saturday November 23 Albion travelled to Goodison Park, where, as the first Football League founder members to visit the ground that season, their shared in Everton's celebrations as the first club to spend a hundred seasons in the top flight. Everton also celebrated with three points that took them above Liverpool into third place in the Premiership.

It took a scrambled goal from substitute Daniel Dichio – his first of the season – to beat a Middlesbrough side that hit the bar twice in the closing stages. Albion would go another nine weeks without a League win after that.

*Nemeth beats Hoult at the Riverside Stadium, one of Middlesbrough's three*

They totally dominated the Sunday afternoon live TV game at White Hart Lane, yet still managed to concede three sloppy goals, although Scott Dobie's consolation effort was one of the best goals scored by an Albion player in the Premiership. Albion deserved nothing from the trip to Villa Park six days later. The home side missed a host of chances, before grabbing all three points, albeit with a deflected shot in the last minute from Hitzlberger.

There was a turning point, of a sort, at the game against Sunderland at The Hawthorns four days before Christmas. The Wearsiders had lost manager Peter Reid, and Howard Wilkinson had taken over, but his side were still bottom of the table, with a terrible record. Albion were two places higher, and really needed to win the 'six-pointer' to move out of the relegation zone before tough games coming up against Arsenal and United. Things looked good when first Dichio and then Koumas put Albion two goals ahead after 32 minutes, but once again, defensive sloppiness allowed Kevin Phillips to score twice to snatch a point.

Only the thickness of a post denied Albion against a strangely lack-lustre Arsenal on Boxing Day. Albion scored first, but let it slip, only for Jason Roberts to crash a shot against the woodwork late in the second half. Right at the death a lucky rebound presented Thierry Henry with the winner.

Two days later, Albion once again controlled a game almost from start to finish, against Charlton at The Valley, but missed chances meant another defeat. Even the weather conspired against the Baggies. On New Year's Day they were due to travel to play injury-hit Fulham at Loftus Road. Tigana's men, slowly slipping down the table, would have been forced to field a scratch side, but the game was called off because of a waterlogged pitch.

The New Year actually started with a comprehensive 3-1 win over First Division Bradford City in the third round of the FA Cup. Albion could have scored six or seven but had to settle for a Daniel Dichio hat-trick – one of just three scored in total between the third round and the Final — which earned them a winnable tie at First Division Watford.

The second round of the Premiership started with a visit from Manchester United. They had won 5-1 in their last visit to The Hawthorns back in 1985-86 and it could have been a similar scoreline once they had got over the shock of conceding an early goal to Jason Koumas. Ruud van Nistelroy took just 22 seconds to put United back in the game, and they ran out easy winners in the end.

*Ifeanyi Udeze — Albion's only signing*

There was more bad luck for the Baggies at Leeds. Albion played well enough, but should have had a penalty when Lucas Radebe clearly handled in the box, to stop Lee Hughes; Andy Johnson was sent off for protesting too much, but Albion still picked up a rare away point.

The following week, they went down ignominiously at Watford in the FA Cup, failing to get a shot on target until added time. The Hornets progressed right to the semi-final before bowing out to Southampton.

Charlton were the next visitors in a midweek game to The Hawthorns; as in the game at The Valley, Albion dominated the game, but failed to get the ball into the net, and went down because of that inadequacy; they had gone nearly six hours without a goal, and dropped into bottom place. That game also marked the closing of the January transfer window, which went by with Albion, unforgivably, making just one loan signing, that of Ifeanyi Udeze, the Nigerian international fullback, from PAOK Salonika. Way too little, way too late…

Just when Albion fans had begun to accept the inevitable, Albion bounced back with their first League win in nine weeks, in what would be their final visit to Maine Road before Manchester City's move to the Commonwealth Stadium in the summer. Both goals – from Clement and Moore – were scored by defenders, and near the end Jason Roberts was harshly sent off for a stray elbow. The win took Albion two places up in the table and set them up perfectly for the home game against rivals Bolton, but despite dominating the game, it needed a late, late equaliser from Andy Johnson to snatch a point. That game, in many ways, was the turning point of the season; not only

did they lose Jason Roberts for three games due to suspension, they had to do without Johnson, who broke his foot in the game, for a month, just after he had returned from a three game suspension. It was more than Albion's meagre resources could cope with.

Four days later Albion took on another struggling side, Fulham, at Loftus Road; the 'game in hand' postponed from New Year's Day. A win would have put Albion back in contention, a point from safety, and for most of the game Albion looking like getting all three points, until a remarkable collapse saw they ship in three goals in eight minutes in the closing stages of the game. Their confidence never recovered, as they went on to lose seven consecutive games at a time when Bolton and West Ham were beginning to start a recovery.

Their next game, in fact, was at home to the Hammers, and the wayward Albion forwards – and Lee Hughes in particular – contrived to miss a series of golden chances to win the game. Trevor Sinclair had three chances, and scored twice to win a game that was generally considered to be a relegation decider, although, of course, in the end, both sides went down.

In their first-ever visit to St Mary's Stadium, Albion went down to another contentious goal, the ball clearly going over the touchline before being put forward for James Beattie – whose personal goal tally for the season was greater than that for the whole Albion side – to poach the winner.

Chelsea – with Zola in glorious form again – won 2-0 at The Hawthorns, and neighbours Blues, who had bought wisely in January, rubbed it in with an injury time winner at St Andrews. Two weeks later Albion went down 3-0 at Middlesbrough, when it could so easily have been seven or eight, and that was followed by another dismal home defeat by an Everton side still looking for a place in the Champions League. At least Albion were awarded their one and only penalty of the season, put away by Igor Balis exactly twelve months to the day that he had scored from the spot at Bradford.

The following week Albion took on Sunderland at the Stadium of Light, in the Relegation Cup Final, with the losers knowing that they would almost certainly end up as the worst side in Premiership history. Albion fully deserved their 2-1 win against the already relegated northerners, thanks to two goals from Derek McInnes. Results elsewhere dictated that, despite the win, Albion's spell back in the top flight was officially at an end.

The only difference between Albion and Tottenham on Easter Monday was the elusive Robbie Keane, who scored twice to rob the Albion of a point, but five days later it was a very different story, as Liverpool came to town. Michael Owen scored four, and Baros two, as Albion went down to the worst home defeat in their history – and to be truthful, they were lucky only to let in six...

At least Albion managed to end the season with a little style, grabbing a point at Euro-chasing Blackburn — a match memorable for the away support all dressing up as referees — and following that up with a last day draw against Champions League side Newcastle United.

Two days later, a dreadful season ended on a celebratory note, when the Albion (with Megson nowhere to be seen) took on a Bryan Robson Select XI at The Hawthorns, for the Bob Taylor Testimonial game. Over 16,000 people turned up to show their appreciation, and see a runaway 7-2 win against a side with the likes of Don Goodman, Sean Flynn and Steve Bull. The previous day, it had been announced that Taylor, along with Udeze, Jordao and Jensen, had been given free transfers, whilst Lee Marshall had been placed on the transfer list.

*Albion's Baggie of The Year, Jason Koumas, left, scores a glorious goal at Ewood Park*

# 2002-03 Friendlies

Albion's choice of pre-season friendlies certainly raised a few eyebrows. After three successive trips to Denmark, the club decided that a low key approach would be the best preparation for their debut in the Premiership.

The warm-up games started with a rarity — two first team games arranged on the same day, just a few miles apart. The smart money was on the game at Bromsgrove, where a side that boasted Dobie and Roberts was far too much for the locals. New Scottish international Dobie bagged a hat-trick, but the Albion's best player was diminutive winger Matt Turner — who never got another chance again. Meanwhile, another pretty strong side went down 2-0 at Halesowen.

Three days later Albion commenced their tour of the West Country with a 3-2 win at Exeter, and followed that up with a low-key 2-0 victory at Tiverton Town.

On the Saturday Albion struggled to beat Torquay United thanks to a solitary goal from Jason Roberts, and they looked anything but Premiership quality when they went down to defeat against Bristol Rovers in their first-ever visit to the Memorial Stadium.

It could have been worse; Rovers, who had narrowly avoided demotion from the League the previous season, were two goals ahead before a late rally saw Albion storm back, only to let in a late winner.

The games continued with two friendlies in the Potteries, a goalless draw at the Britannia Stadium, in which Megson gave a brief trial to Ajax full-back Tim de Cler, and a 2-1 win at Vale Park — another game where Albion had to come back from behind against inferior opposition.

A week before they opened their season proper against Manchester United at Old Trafford, Albion bizarrely lined up against Stevenage, and although they won 4-0, they were hardly convincing.

There were no friendlies during the rest of the season, but the campaign was concluded on May 13 with the Bob Taylor Testimonial game, against a Bryan Robson Select XI — comprised almost entirely of ex-Albion players, the likes of Steve Bull, the Robson brothers, Don Goodman, Richard Sneekes and Sean Flynn. Taylor scored twice, as did Andy Johnson, as the goals flowed for the only time all season, with the current Albion side beating the oldsters 7-2 in front of 16,017 fans.

*Attendance: 2,158*
*Referee: D Satterthwaite (Bromsgrove)*
*Assistants: R Baker & M Cunningham*

# BROMSGROVE 1    ALBION 6

Burgess 69

*Dobie 19, 23,79 Roberts 25, 32*
*Turner 43*

| | | |
|---|---|---|
| Matt LOWE [77] | 1 | Russell HOULT [69] |
| Paul LLOYD [60] | 2 | Igor BALIS |
| Kevin BANNER | 3 | Lloyd DYER |
| Steve POPE | 4 | Ronnie WALLWORK |
| John FORD [55] | 5 | Tony BUTLER |
| Stewart BRIGHTON | 6 | Phil GILCHRIST |
| Mark CRISP [55] | 7 | Derek McINNES |
| Steve TAYLOR [55] | 8 | Adam CHAMBERS |
| Les PALMER [60] | 9 | Matt TURNER |
| Paul DANKS [60] | 10 | Scott DOBIE |
| Grant BECKETT | 11 | Jason ROBERTS |
| Steve THOMAS [77] | 12 | Tamika MKANDAWIRE [60] |
| Steve FROST [55] | 13 | Joe MURPHY [69] |
| Mark CLIFTON [55] | 14 | |
| Richard BURGESS [60] | 15 | |
| James DYSON [55] | 16 | |
| Ian PORTER [60] | | |
| Ashley READ [60] | | |

## THE MATCH IN BRIEF

A great start for the newly promoted Baggies with a superb pre-
season display at the Victoria
Ground, Bromsgrove. Dobie
scores a hat-trick, but the real
star is young Matt Turner *Right:*
*Dobie's first goal*

*93*

*Attendance: 1,727*
*Referee: M Fletcher (Warley)*
*Assistants:*

# HALESOWEN 2   ALBION 0

*A Jones 4, M Taylor 42*

| | | |
|---|---|---|
| Tim CLARKE | 1 | Brian JENSEN |
| Richard COLWELL [HT] | 2 | Des LYTTLE |
| Lee COLLINS [HT] | 3 | Neil CLEMENT |
| Jason BURNHAM [71] | 4 | Matt COLLINS |
| Neil SMITH [62] | 5 | Darren MOORE |
| Andrew SPENCER [71] | 6 | Larus SIGURDSSON |
| Stuart SKIDMORE [75] | 7 | Andy JOHNSON |
| Mark TAYLOR [HT] | 8 | JORDAO |
| Leslie HINES | 9 | Daniel DICHIO [56] |
| Rob ELMES [62] | 10 | Bob TAYLOR |
| Andy JONES [HT] | 11 | James CHAMBERS |
| ASHBY [HT] | 12 | Mark BRIGGS [56] |
| Sean FLYNN [HT] | 13 | Chris ADAMSON |
| Paul REECE [71] | 14 | Ross ADAMS |
| Dave BARNETT [62] | 15 | |
| Jimmy QUIGGIN [71] | 16 | |
| Richard ADAMS [75] | 17 | |
| Ross COLLINS [HT] | 18 | |
| Richard LEADBEATER [62] | 19 | |
| John NEWALL [HT] | 20 | |

## THE MATCH IN BRIEF

There is a huge contrast between the performances at Bromsgrove and Halesowen, as another, potentially very strong Albion side goes down 2-0 without much of a fight at The Grove. Andy Johnson and youngster Matt Collins (above) are the only players to shine...

*Attendance: 2,354*
*Referee:  P Rejer (Worcs)*
*Assistants:M Mullarkey & N Jones*

# EXETER CITY 2             ALBION 3
*Flack 14, McConnell 79 pen*        *Dichio 21, Roberts 26,*
                                    *Balis 59 pen*

| | | |
|---|---|---|
| Arjan van HEUSEN | 1 | Russell HOULT |
| Graeme POWER | 2 | Igor BALIS |
| Justin WALKER  [57] | 3 | Neil CLEMENT |
| Andy ROSCOE  [52] | 4 | Derek McINNES |
| Steve FLACK  [67] | 5 | Darren MOORE |
| Barry McCONNELL | 6 | Larus SIGURDSSON |
| Martin THOMAS | 7 | Ronnie WALLWORK |
| Alex WATSON  [64] | 8 | Lloyd DYER |
| Santos GAIA | 9 | Daniel DICHIO |
| Glen CRONIN  [69] | 10 | Andy JOHNSON |
| James COPPINGER  [84] | 11 | Jason ROBERTS [50] |
| Kwame AMPADU | 12 | Scott DOBIE [50] |
| Sean McCARTHY  [67] | 13 | Bob TAYLOR |
| Geoff BRESLAN  [69] | 14 | Adam CHAMBERS |
| Mark BURROWS | 15 | James CHAMBERS |
| Gareth SHELDON  [52] | 16 | JORDAO |
| Les AFFUL  [84] | 17 | Brian JENSEN |
| Stuart FRASER | 18 | Joe MURPHY |
| Jamie EDWARDS  [57] | 19 | |
| Tom JORDAN  [64] | 20 | |
| Sean GOFF | 21 | |
| Rojas SEGARA | 22 | |

## THE MATCH IN BRIEF
A competitive start to Albion's four game tour of the West Country

*Attendance: 1,370*
*Referee: C Wilkes (Gloucester)*
*Assistants: R Greenwood & I Ansell*

# TIVERTON 0     ALBION 2

*McInnes 69, Taylor 79*

| | | |
|---|---|---|
| John VAUGHAN | 1 | Joe MURPHY [HT] |
| Steve WINTER [81] | 2 | James CHAMBERS |
| Danny HAINES [65] | 3 | Neil CLEMENT |
| Steve PETERS | 4 | Derek McINNES |
| Nathan RUDGE | 5 | Darren MOORE |
| Rob COUSINS | 6 | Adam CHAMBERS |
| David STEELE | 7 | Ronnie WALLWORK |
| Jason REES | 8 | Lloyd DYER [62] |
| Phil EVERETT | 9 | Bob TAYLOR |
| Scott ROGERS | 10 | Scott DOBIE |
| Jamie MUDGE | 11 | JORDAO [57] |
| Luke VINNICOMBE [81] | 12 | Larus SIGURDSSON [62] |
| Richard PEARS [65] | 13 | Brian JENSEN [HT] |
| Anthony LYNCH [67] | 14 | Igor BALIS |
| Steve OWENS | 15 | Jason ROBERTS |
| Kevin NANCEKIVELL | 16 | Daniel DICHIO |
| Steve GROSS | 17 | Andy JOHNSON [57] |

## THE MATCH IN BRIEF

Another competitive game against Dr Martens Premier League side Tiverton at Ladysmead. It takes two late goals, from McInnes and Taylor to prevent a great deal of embarrassment, as the non-League side goes close to pulling off a surprise win against the newly promoted Baggies

*Attendance: 2,675*
*Referee: P Rejer (Worcs)*
*Assistants: N Jones & I Harris*

# TORQUAY U 0     ALBION 1
*Roberts 28*

| | | |
|---|---|---|
| Kevin DEARDEN | 1 | Russell HOULT |
| Reuben HAZELL [60] | 2 | Igor BALIS |
| David WOOZLEY [74] | 3 | Neil CLEMENT [HT] |
| Sean HANKIN [72] | 4 | Derek McINNES |
| Lee CANOVILLE | 5 | Darren MOORE |
| Alex RUSSELL [60] | 6 | Adam CHAMBERS |
| Kevin HILL [72] | 7 | Ronnie WALLWORK |
| Jason FOWLER [52] | 8 | Larus SIGURDSSON |
| Tony BEDEAU [72] | 9 | Scott DOBIE |
| David GRAHAM [72] | 10 | Andy JOHNSON |
| Marcus RICHARDSON [70] | 11 | Jason ROBERTS [60] |
| Ryan ASHINGTON [60] | 12 | Bob TAYLOR |
| Charles ADYE [74] | 13 | Brian JENSEN |
| Michael SMALL [72] | 14 | Lloyd DYER [HT] |
| Troy DOUGHLIN [60] | 15 | Joe MURPHY |
| Kelechi OKORIE [72] | 16 | Daniel DICHIO [60] |
| Matt HOCKLEY [52] | 17 | James CHAMBERS |
| Chad NARAGHI | 18 | JORDAO |
| Dean STEVENS [70] | 19 | |
| Ryan NORTHMORE | 20 | |
| David CARNS | 21 | |
| Jamie ATTWELL | 22 | |
| Lucas BURGESS [72] | 23 | |

Attendance: 4,063
Referee: P Rejer (Worcs)
Assistants: S Bratt & K Townsend

# BRISTOL R 3    ALBION 2
*Graziolli 41, 60, Gilroy 82*    *Wallwork 72, Dichio 74*

| Bristol R | No. | Albion |
|---|---|---|
| Scott HOWIE | 1 | Brian JENSEN |
| Danny BOXALL | 2 | Igor BALIS |
| Trevor CHALLIS | 3 | Neil CLEMENT |
| Simon BRYANT [70] | 4 | Derek McINNES |
| Anwar UDDIN | 5 | Darren MOORE |
| Adam BARRETT | 6 | James CHAMBERS |
| Wayne CARLISLE | 7 | Ronnie WALLWORK |
| Robert QUINN | 8 | Adam CHAMBERS [HT] |
| Paul TAIT | 9 | Daniel DICHIO |
| Guiliano GRAZIOLI [74] | 10 | Andy JOHNSON |
| Vitalijs ASTAFJEVS | 11 | Scott DOBIE [HT] |
| Lewis HOGG | 12 | Larus SIGURDSSON [HT] |
| Ryan CLARKE | 13 | Jason ROBERTS [HT] |
| Mark McKEEVER [HT] | 14 | Bob TAYLOR |
| David GILROY [74] | 15 | Lloyd DYER |
| Justin RICHARDS | 16 | Joe MURPHY |
| Drew SHORE | 17 | RUSSELL HOULT |
| Rob SCOTT | 18 | JORDAO |
| Kevin GALL | 19 | |
| Vitalijs ASTAFJEVS [70] | 20 | |

## THE MATCH IN BRIEF
Although Albion stage a brief comeback to draw level after being
two goals down in their first visit to the Memorial Stadium,
another defensive error allows substitute Dave Gilroy to plunder
a late winner for the Third Division side

98

*Attendance: 6,241*
*Referee:  P Dowd (Stoke)*
*Assistants: RL Lewis & N Hancox*

# STOKE CITY 0      ALBION 0

| | | |
|---|---|---|
| Neil CUTLER | 1 | Russell HOULT |
| Wayne THOMAS | 2 | Igor BALIS [70] |
| Kris COMMONS [57] | 3 | Neil CLEMENT [55] |
| Peter HANDYSIDE | 4 | Derek McINNES |
| Sergei SHTANIUK | 5 | Darren MOORE |
| Karl HENRY | 6 | Larus SIGURDSSON |
| James O'CONNOR | 7 | Ronnie WALLWORK |
| Bjarni GUDJONSSON[71] | 8 | Adam CHAMBERS [55] |
| Chris IWELUMO [68] | 9 | Daniel DICHIO [HT] |
| Chris GREENACRE | 10 | Andy JOHNSON |
| Lewis NEAL | 11 | Jason ROBERTS |
| Andy COOKE | 12 | Scott DOBIE [HT] |
| Brian WILSON | 13 | Bob TAYLOR |
| Marc GOODFELLOW[68] | 14 | JORDAO [55] |
| David ROWSON [57] | 15 | James CHAMBERS [70] |
| Petur MARTEINSSON | 16 | Tim DE CLER [55] |
| Bryn GUNNARSSON [71] | 17 | Brian JENSEN |
| Jani VIANDER | 18 | Joe MURPHY |
| | 19 | |

## THE MATCH IN BRIEF
An uninspiring display for the Albion, as they meet their
toughest pre-season opposition in the form of First Division
Stoke City, at the Britannia Stadium. The Premiership side
misses the best chance to win it, but a goalless draw is about
right after a tedious 90 minutes in the Potteries.

*Attendance: 2,282*
*Referee: Mark Warren (Walsall)*
*Assistants: R Burton & G A Aston*

## PORT VALE 1     ALBION 2

*Boyd 24*           *Johnson 27, Balis 55 pen*

| | | |
|---|---|---|
| DEAN DELANEY | 1 | Russell HOULT |
| Ian BRIGHTWELL [HT] | 2 | Igor BALIS |
| Phil CHARNOCK | 3 | Neil CLEMENT |
| Mark BOYD [HT] | 4 | Derek McINNES [80] |
| Michael WALSH [65] | 5 | Darren MOORE |
| Sam COLLINS | 6 | Phil GILCHRIST |
| Michael CUMMINS | 7 | Ronnie WALLWORK |
| Marc BRIDGE-WILKINSON[65] | 8 | Larus SIGURDSSON |
| Stephen BROOKER | 9 | Scott DOBIE [60] |
| Brett ANGEL [65] | 10 | Andy JOHNSON |
| John DURNIN [HT] | 11 | Jason ROBERTS |
| Neil BRISCO [HT] | 12 | Adam CHAMBERS [80] |
| Matt CARRAGHER [HT] | 13 | Bob TAYLOR [60] |
| Ian ARMSTRONG [65] | 14 | JORDAO |
| Rae INGRAM [65] | 15 | James CHAMBERS |
| Sean McCLARE [65] | 16 | Tim DE CLER |
| Jon McCARTHY [HT] | 17 | Brian JENSEN |
| Steve ROWLAND | 18 | Joe MURPHY |
| Billy PAYNTER | 19 | |
| Liam BURNS | 20 | |

### THE MATCH IN BRIEF

There was no second chance for triallist Tim de Cler as Albion won at Vale Park against a poor looking Second Division side

*Attendance: 1,539*
*Referee: Steve Chittenden (Herts)*
*Assistants: A Parker & A Stevens*

# STEVENAGE B. 0  ALBION 4

*Dichio 38, Johnson 40*
*Taylor 81, Clement 83*

| | | |
|---|---|---|
| Russell HOULT | 1 | Mark WESTHEAD |
| Igor BALIS | 2 | Simon TRAVIS |
| Neil CLEMENT | 3 | Jamie CAMPBELL |
| Derek McINNES | 4 | Matt FISHER  [79] |
| Darren MOORE [HT] | 5 | Jason GOODLIFFE [69] |
| Phil GILCHRIST | 6 | Jude STIRLING |
| Sean GREGAN | 7 | Simon WORMULL |
| Larus SIGURDSSON | 8 | Jon CULLEN |
| Daniel DICHIO [66] | 9 | Kirk JACKSON [76] |
| Andy JOHNSON | 10 | Jean Michel SIGERE [62] |
| Jason ROBERTS | 11 | Scott HOUGHTON |
| Ronnie WALLWORK[HT] | 12 | Adrian CLARKE |
| Bob TAYLOR [66] | 13 | Phil WILSON |
| Scott DOBIE [HT] | 14 | |
| Adam CHAMBERS | 15 | |
| James CHAMBERS | 16 | |
| Brian JENSEN | 17 | |
| Joe MURPHY | 18 | |

## THE MATCH IN BRIEF
It seemed to be a strange final warm-up game for a season
in the Premiership, but Albion saw off Conference side
Stevenage Borough without too much trouble, in a game
that also saw the last goal that Bob Taylor would ever score
in an Albion shirt — until his Testimonial game...

*Attendance: 16,017*
*Referee: Paul Rejer (Worcs)*
*Assistants: J Smith & M Smith*

## ALBION 7     B. ROBSON XI 2

*Taylor 8, 90 pen, McInnes 29*    *Hamilton 45, G Robson 47*
*Johnson 36,37, Roberts 17, Brown 75*

| | | |
|---|---|---|
| Russell HOULT [HT] | 1 | Tim FLOWERS [HT] |
| James CHAMBERS | 2 | Ian HAMILTON [72] |
| Neil CLEMENT [84] | 3 | John TREWICK [72] |
| Derek McINNES [61] | 4 | Carlton PALMER |
| Larus SIGURDSSON [HT] | 5 | Ross ADAMS |
| Des LYTTLE [51] | 6 | Gary ROBSON |
| Ronnie WALLWORK[HT][51] | 7 | Bryan ROBSON [77] |
| Jason ROBERTS [HT] [76] | 8 | Richard SNEEKES |
| Bob TAYLOR [22] [80] | 9 | Steve BULL [HT] |
| Andy JOHNSON [HT] | 10 | Don GOODMAN [77] |
| Jason KOUMAS [76] | 11 | Sean FLYNN [72] |
| Lloyd DYER [HT] | 12 | Wayne FEREDAY [72] |
| Simon BROWN [HT] | 13 | Brian JENSEN [HT] |
| Matthew COLLINS [HT] | 14 | Garry HACKETT [72] |
| Scott DOBIE [HT] | 15 | Richard O'KELLY [77] |
| Daniel CRANE [HT] [80] | 16 | Lee HUGHES [HT] |
| Andy TIERNAN [61] | 17 | Cyrille REGIS [77] |
| Lee HUGHES [22] [HT] | 18 | Steve LILWALL [72] |
| Ken HIPKISS [84] | 19 | |
| Tamika MKANDAWIRE [HT] | 20 | |

### THE MATCH IN BRIEF

Over 16,000 paid to see Bob Taylor's testimonial game
against an ex-Albion side assembled by Bryan Robson. At
least they got to see their side score seven goals — with a bit
of assistance from referee (and Albion fan) Paul Rejer.

# PLAYERS' APPEARANCES & GOALS 2002-03

| | Premier | WC | FAC | Others |
|---|---|---|---|---|
| Russell Hoult | 37 | - | 2 | 7 |
| Sean Gregan | 36(1) | - | 2 | 1 |
| Neil Clement | 34+2(3) | 0+1 | 2 | 9(1) |
| Jason Roberts | 31+1(3) | - | 2 | 7+1(5) |
| Andy Johnson | 30+2(1) | - | 2 | 8+1(4) |
| Darren Moore | 29 (2) | - | 2 | 8 |
| Derek McInnes | 28+1(2) | - | 1 | 9(2) |
| Jason Koumas | 27+5(4) | 1 | 2 | 1 |
| Igor Balis | 27+1(2) | - | 0+1 | 7(2) |
| Larus Sigurdsson | 23+6 | 1 | 1+1 | 7+2 |
| Ronnie Wallwork | 23+4 | 1 | 2 | 8+1(1) |
| Phil Gilchrist | 22 | - | 1+1 | 3 |
| Daniel Dichio | 19+9(5) | - | 1+1(3) | 5+1(3) |
| Lee Hughes | 14+9 | 1(1) | - | 0+1 |
| Scott Dobie | 10+21(5) | 0+1 | 0+2 | 5+4(3) |
| Adam Chambers | 10+3 | - | 1+1 | 5+1 |
| Ifeanyi Udeze | 7+4 | - | - | - |
| Lee Marshall | 4+5(1) | 1 | - | - |
| James Chambers | 2+6 | 1 | - | 4+1 |
| Bob Taylor | 2+2 | - | - | 3+2(4) |
| Des Lyttle | 2+2 | 1 | - | 2 |
| Joe Murphy | 1+1 | 1 | - | 1+1 |
| Jordao | 0+3 | 1 | - | 2+1 |
| Lloyd Dyer | - | 1 | - | 3+2 |
| Brian Jensen | - | - | - | 2+1 |
| Matthew Collins | - | - | - | 1+1 |
| Tony Butler | - | - | - | 1 |
| Matt Turner | - | - | - | 1(1) |
| Tamika Mkandawire | - | - | - | 0+2 |
| Mark Briggs | - | - | - | 0+1 |
| Tim de Cler | - | - | - | 0+1 |
| Daniel Crane | - | - | - | 0+1 |
| Simon Brown | - | - | - | 0+1(1) |
| Andy Tiernan | - | - | - | 0+1 |
| Rev. Ken Hipkiss | - | - | - | 0+1 |

*WC: Worthington Cup, FAC: FA Cup "Others" include all pre-season games, plus the Bob Taylor Testimonial.*

# THE PREMIERSHIP 2002-03

|       |    |                          |      |                        | Position |
|-------|----|--------------------------|------|------------------------|----------|
| Aug   | 17 | A Man Utd                | 0-1  | —                      | 18       |
|       | 24 | **H Leeds Utd**          | 1-3  | *Marshall*             | 18       |
|       | 27 | A Arsenal                | 2-5  | *Roberts, Dobie*       | 20       |
|       | 31 | **H Fulham**             | 1-0  | *Moore*                | 17       |
| Sep   | 11 | A West Ham               | 1-0  | *Roberts*              | 13       |
|       | 14 | **H Southampton**        | 1-0  | *Gregan*               | 7        |
|       | 21 | A Liverpool              | 0-2  | —                      | 10       |
|       | 30 | **H Blackburn**          | 0-2  | —                      | 13       |
| Oct   | 2  | *A Wigan Ath (WC)*       | 1-3  | *Hughes*               | -        |
|       | 5  | A Newcastle              | 1-2  | *Balis*                | 13       |
|       | 19 | **H Birmingham C**       | 1-1  | *Roberts*              | 15       |
|       | 26 | A Chelsea                | 0-2  | —                      | 18       |
| Nov   | 2  | **H Man City**           | 1-2  | *Clement*              | 18       |
|       | 9  | A Bolton W               | 1-1  | *Dobie*                | 18       |
|       | 16 | **H Aston Villa**        | 0-0  | —                      | 19       |
|       | 23 | A Everton                | 0-1  | —                      | 19       |
|       | 30 | **H Middlesbrough**      | 1-0  | *Dichio*               | 17       |
| Dec   | 7  | A Tottenham H            | 1-3  | *Dobie*                | 17       |
|       | 14 | A Aston Villa            | 1-2  | *Koumas*               | 18       |
|       | 21 | **H Sunderland**         | 2-2  | *Dichio, Koumas*       | 19       |
|       | 26 | **H Arsenal**            | 1-2  | *Dichio*               | 19       |
|       | 28 | A Charlton A             | 0-1  | —                      | 19       |
| Jan   | 4  | *H Bradford City (FAC3)* | 3-1  | *Dichio 3*             | -        |
|       | 11 | **H Man Utd**            | 1-3  | *Koumas*               | 20       |
|       | 18 | A Leeds Utd              | 0-0  | —                      | 19       |
|       | 25 | *A Watford (FAC4)*       | 0-1  | —                      | -        |
|       | 29 | **H Charlton**           | 0-1  | —                      | 20       |
| Feb   | 1  | A Man City               | 2-1  | *Clement, Moore*       | 18       |
|       | 8  | **H Bolton W**           | 1-1  | *Johnson*              | 18       |
|       | 19 | A Fulham                 | 0-3  | —                      | 18       |
|       | 23 | **H West Ham**           | 1-2  | *Dichio*               | 19       |
| Mar   | 1  | A Southampton            | 0-1  | —                      | 19       |
|       | 16 | **H Chelsea**            | 0-2  | —                      | 19       |
|       | 22 | A Birmingham             | 0-1  | —                      | 19       |
| Apr   | 5  | A Middlesbrough          | 0-3  | —                      | 19       |
|       | 12 | **H Everton**            | 1-2  | *Balis [pen]*          | 19       |
|       | 19 | A Sunderland             | 2-1  | *McInnes 2*            | 19       |
|       | 21 | **H Tottenham**          | 2-3  | *Dichio, Clement*      | 19       |
|       | 26 | **H Liverpool**          | 0-6  | —                      | 19       |
| May   | 3  | A Blackburn R            | 1-1  | *Koumas*               | 19       |
|       | 11 | **H Newcastle U**        | 2-2  | *Dobie 2*              | 19       |
|       | 13 | ***H B Robson XI** (Test)* | 7-2 | *Taylor 2 [1 pen], Johnson 2, Roberts, McInnes, Brown* |  |

# THE PREMIERSHIP 2002-03

|    |              |    | **Home** | | | | | **Away** | | | | |
|----|--------------|----|----|----|----|----|----|----|----|----|----|-----|
|    |              | P  | W  | D  | L  | F  | A  | W  | D  | L  | F  | A  | Pts |
| 1.  | Manchester U   | 38 | 16 | 2 | 1  | 42 | 12 | 9 | 6 | 4  | 32 | 22 | 83 |
| 2.  | Arsenal        | 38 | 15 | 2 | 2  | 47 | 20 | 8 | 7 | 4  | 38 | 22 | 78 |
| 3.  | Newcastle U    | 38 | 15 | 2 | 2  | 36 | 17 | 6 | 4 | 9  | 31 | 15 | 69 |
| 4.  | Chelsea        | 38 | 12 | 5 | 2  | 41 | 15 | 7 | 5 | 7  | 27 | 23 | 67 |
| 5.  | Liverpool      | 38 | 9  | 8 | 2  | 30 | 16 | 9 | 2 | 8  | 31 | 25 | 64 |
| 6.  | Blackburn R    | 38 | 9  | 7 | 3  | 24 | 15 | 7 | 5 | 7  | 28 | 28 | 60 |
| 7.  | Everton        | 38 | 11 | 5 | 3  | 28 | 19 | 6 | 3 | 10 | 20 | 30 | 59 |
| 8.  | Southampton    | 38 | 9  | 8 | 2  | 25 | 16 | 4 | 5 | 10 | 18 | 30 | 52 |
| 9.  | Manchester C   | 38 | 9  | 2 | 8  | 28 | 26 | 6 | 4 | 9  | 19 | 28 | 51 |
| 10. | Tottenham H    | 38 | 9  | 4 | 6  | 30 | 29 | 5 | 4 | 10 | 21 | 33 | 50 |
| 11. | Middlesbrough  | 38 | 10 | 7 | 2  | 36 | 21 | 3 | 3 | 13 | 12 | 23 | 49 |
| 12. | Charlton A.    | 38 | 8  | 3 | 8  | 26 | 30 | 6 | 4 | 9  | 19 | 26 | 49 |
| 13. | Birmingham     | 38 | 8  | 5 | 6  | 25 | 23 | 5 | 4 | 10 | 16 | 26 | 48 |
| 14. | Fulham         | 38 | 11 | 3 | 5  | 26 | 18 | 2 | 6 | 11 | 15 | 32 | 48 |
| 15. | Leeds United   | 38 | 7  | 3 | 9  | 25 | 26 | 7 | 2 | 10 | 33 | 31 | 47 |
| 16. | Aston Villa    | 38 | 11 | 2 | 6  | 25 | 14 | 1 | 7 | 11 | 17 | 33 | 45 |
| 17. | Bolton W.      | 38 | 7  | 8 | 4  | 27 | 24 | 3 | 6 | 10 | 14 | 27 | 44 |
| 18. | West Ham U.    | 38 | 5  | 7 | 7  | 21 | 24 | 5 | 5 | 9  | 21 | 35 | 42 |
| **19.** | **Albion** | **38** | **3** | **5** | **11** | **17** | **34** | **3** | **3** | **13** | **12** | **31** | **26** |
| 20. | Sunderland     | 38 | 3  | 2 | 14 | 11 | 31 | 1 | 5 | 13 | 10 | 34 | 19 |

## RELEGATED

*Albion, West Ham and Sunderland  Sunderland's total of 19 points is a new low for the Premiership. Champions League: Manchester United, Arsenal, Newcastle & Chelsea UEFA Cup: Liverpool & Blackburn*

### PREMIERSHIP RESERVE (NORTH)

|              | P  | W  | D  | L  | F  | A  | GD  | Pts |
|--------------|----|----|----|----|----|----|-----|-----|
| Sunderland   | 28 | 17 | 4  | 7  | 51 | 26 | 25  | 55  |
| Midd'boro    | 28 | 16 | 7  | 5  | 47 | 26 | 21  | 55  |
| Man City     | 28 | 17 | 3  | 8  | 55 | 27 | 28  | 54  |
| Aston Villa  | 28 | 16 | 4  | 8  | 59 | 44 | 15  | 52  |
| Liverpool    | 28 | 13 | 5  | 10 | 48 | 34 | 14  | 44  |
| Everton      | 28 | 12 | 7  | 9  | 44 | 36 | 8   | 43  |
| Leeds U      | 28 | 10 | 11 | 7  | 45 | 37 | 8   | 41  |
| Man Utd      | 28 | 12 | 5  | 11 | 45 | 37 | 8   | 41  |
| Bolton       | 28 | 11 | 5  | 12 | 45 | 48 | -3  | 38  |
| Birmingham C | 28 | 11 | 4  | 13 | 33 | 39 | -6  | 37  |
| **Albion**   | **28** | **8** | **11** | **9** | **27** | **31** | **-4** | **35** |
| Newcastle    | 28 | 8  | 9  | 11 | 44 | 43 | 1   | 33  |
| Blackburn R  | 28 | 10 | 3  | 15 | 34 | 51 | -17 | 33  |
| Sheff Wed    | 28 | 3  | 5  | 20 | 21 | 55 | -34 | 14  |
| Bradford C   | 28 | 3  | 3  | 22 | 20 | 84 | -64 | 12  |

### YOUTH ALLIANCE MIDLAND

|              | P  | W  | D  | L  | F  | A  | Pts |
|--------------|----|----|----|----|----|----|-----|
| **Albion**   | **16** | **10** | **2** | **4** | **31** | **20** | **32** |
| Northmpton   | 16 | 11 | 5 | 4 | 21 | 13 | 30 |
| Peterboro'   | 15 | 9  | 0 | 6 | 36 | 16 | 27 |
| Cambridge U  | 15 | 7  | 3 | 5 | 25 | 19 | 24 |
| Oxford U     | 15 | 8  | 0 | 7 | 21 | 28 | 24 |
| Luton T      | 14 | 7  | 2 | 5 | 19 | 14 | 23 |
| Walsall      | 15 | 6  | 2 | 7 | 27 | 25 | 20 |
| Kiddermster  | 14 | 3  | 1 | 10 | 19 | 38 | 10 |
| Rushden & D  | 16 | 1  | 3 | 12 | 16 | 42 | 6 |

### DIVISION ONE SOUTH

|               | P  | W  | D  | L  | F  | A  | Pts |
|---------------|----|----|----|----|----|----|-----|
| Brentford     | 9  | 5  | 4  | 0  | 18 | 12 | 19 |
| Northampton   | 9  | 3  | 6  | 0  | 14 | 11 | 15 |
| Cardiff City  | 9  | 3  | 5  | 1  | 14 | 13 | 14 |
| Plymouth A    | 9  | 3  | 4  | 2  | 14 | 9  | 13 |
| **Albion**    | **9** | **3** | **4** | **2** | **13** | **12** | **13** |
| Bristol R     | 9  | 3  | 1  | 5  | 12 | 18 | 10 |
| Peterborough  | 9  | 1  | 6  | 2  | 13 | 14 | 9 |
| Swindon Town  | 9  | 2  | 3  | 4  | 10 | 13 | 9 |
| Portsmouth    | 9  | 2  | 2  | 5  | 9  | 12 | 8 |
| Wycombe W     | 9  | 1  | 3  | 5  | 6  | 9  | 6 |

# PREMIER (North) 2002-03

| | | | | |
|---|---|---|---|---|
| *Aug* | 21 | A Man United | 0-1 | — |
| *Sep* | 2 | **H Birmingham C** | 3-0 | *Turner, Dichio, Taylor* |
| | 16 | **H Bolton W** | 1-0 | *Taylor* |
| | 26 | A Sheff Wed | 2-0 | *J Chambers, Turner* |
| *Oct* | 7 | **H Newcastle U** | 0-0 | — |
| | 21 | **H Everton** | 2-2 | *Dobie (2)* |
| | 28 | **H Man City** | 1-2 | *Hughes* |
| *Nov* | 11 | A Sunderland | 0-2 | — |
| | 18 | **H Bradford City** | 4-0 | *Jordao, Marshall, Hughes, Dichio* |
| | 25 | A Liverpool | 1-3 | *Dichio* |
| *Dec* | 4 | A Leeds United | 1-1 | *Collins* |
| | 10 | A Middlesbrough | 0-0 | — |
| | 18 | **H Blackburn R** | 0-1 | — |
| *Jan* | 7 | A Aston Villa | 2-2 | *Dobie, Mkandawire* |
| | 13 | **H Leeds Utd** | 0-0 | — |
| | 22 | A Birmingham | 0-0 | — |
| *Feb* | 3 | **H Man United** | 1-3 | *Marshall* |
| | 10 | A Bolton W | 2-1 | *Carey-Bertram, Mkandawire* |
| | 24 | A Newcastle | 1-5 | *Jordao* |
| *Mar* | 11 | A Everton | 1-1 | *Taylor* |
| | 17 | **H Sunderland** | 1-0 | *Dyer* |
| | 25 | A Man City | 1-1 | *Brown* |
| *Apr* | 1 | **H Liverpool** | 0-2 | — |
| | 8 | A Bradford City | 0-0 | — |
| | 14 | **H Middlesbrough** | 1-0 | *Carey-Bertram* |
| | 16 | **H Sheff Wed** | 0-3 | — |
| | 22 | A Blackburn R | 0-0 | — |
| | 28 | **H Aston Villa** | 2-1 | *Carey-Bertram* |
| | | | | *Taylor [pen]* |

Appearances *(Premiership Reserves League): Dyer 26+1, Mkandawire 26, J Chambers 25, Lyttle 23, Marshall 21, Jordao, 20, Taylor 18, Collins 14+6, Adams 13+3, Jensen 13+1, Brown 11+2, Murphy 11, Bertram 10+3, Dobie 9, Turner 8+1, Hughes 8, Dichio 7, Crane 4, Warner 3+4, Midworth 3+2, A Chambers 5, Koumas 4, Wallwork 4, Sigurdsson 3, Balis 3, Udeze 3, Briggs 2+2, Gowling 2+1, Appleton 1+1, Patterson 1+1, McInnes, Gregan, Butler 1, Gilchrist 1, Johnson 1, Roberts 1, Willetts 1, Cudworth 0+2, Sherwood 0+1* **Goals:** *Taylor 4, Dobie 4, Dichio 3, Mkandawire 2, Carey-Bertram 2, Marshall 2, Jordao 2, Turner 2, Hughes 2, Collins 1, Brown 1, J Chambers 1* **Appearances** *(BSC): Crane, Warmer, Carey-Bertram, Cudworth, Smikle, Attewell, Clarke, Tomlinson, McHugh, Patterson, Gowling (all 1) Sherwood, Midworth (both 0+1)* **Goal:** *Carey-Bertram*

## BASS CHARITY VASE

| | | | | |
|---|---|---|---|---|
| *July* | 26 | N Gresley | 1-0 | *Carey-Bertram* |
| | 29 | N Nott'm F | 1-1 | *Brown* |
| | | | | (Lost on drawing of lots) |

## BIRMINGHAM SENIOR CUP

| | | | | | |
|---|---|---|---|---|---|
| *Feb* | 11 | *A Tamworth* | 1-1 | *Carey-Bertram* | (Lost 3-4 on pens) |

# RESERVES 2002-03

The Albion Reserve side broke new ground in 2002-03, in that they competed in a new competition – The Premiership Reserve League (North) — for the first time since moving from the Birmingham & District League to the Central League in 1921. It may well be a short stay, as teams will in future be automatically relegated after two years if their club is no longer a member of the Premiership...

Like the first team, the Reserves started at Old Trafford – and went down to a solitary second half goal. It was a very young Albion side representing Albion that day; a stronger line-up went on to win the next three games, against Birmingham, Bolton and Sheffield Wednesday, and by the time Albion entertained Manchester City at the end of October, Albion, against all the odds, were in a challenging position for the title. Eight games without a win put paid to that forlorn dream

The youngsters continued to do well away from home, getting draws against very strong opposition at Leeds, Everton, Manchester City and Blackburn, but they failed badly at home, once they had switched their home game to The Grove, home of Halesowen Town. Of the nine games played there, they won just one, and that against the worst team in the League, Bradford City. In their games at The Hawthorns they won five out of seven; indeed, the Reserves have won just five out of thirty games that they have played at The Grove in recent years.

The worst defeat of the season was a 5-1 thrashing by a very experienced Newcastle side, at Kingston Park. The best performances were three end of season wins at The Hawthorns, as the side beat each of the three championship contenders, Sunderland, Middlesbrough and, memorably, Aston Villa. The latter victory, with goals from Daniel Carey-Bertram and, his last in a competitive game for the club, Bob Taylor, ensured that Villa would miss out on the title.

After reaching the Birmingham Senior Cup Final the year before, Albion effectively put out a youth side again this year, and went out gallantly, on penalties, to a Tamworth side that ran away with promotion to the Conference.

In the pre-season Bass Charity Vase, Albion beat Gresley, but went out on the drawing of lots after a 1-1 draw against Nottingham Forest, who had beaten them in last year's final.

*Carey-Bertram goes close against Middlesbrough at Billingham*

# YOUTHS 2002-03

## Youth Alliance Midland League

| | | | | |
|---|---|---|---|---|
| *Aug* | 24 | A Northampton | 3-2 | *Bertram, Cudworth, Attewell* |
| *Sept* | 28 | **H Peterborough** | 2-1 | *Smikle, Clarke* |
| *Oct* | 5 | A Oxford U | 2-0 | *Bertram, Brown* |
| | 12 | **H Cambridge U** | 2-0 | *Bertram, Gowling* |
| | 19 | **H Luton T** | 1-0 | *Bertram* |
| | 26 | A Walsall | 2-2 | *Bertram, Patterson* |
| *Nov* | 2 | A Rushden & D | 0-1 | — |
| | 16 | A Cambridge U | 2-0 | *Bertram, Gowling* |
| | 23 | **H Oxford U** | 3-2 | *Brown 2, Smikle* |
| | 30 | **H Luton T** | 1-2 | *Patterson* |
| *Dec* | 7 | **H Walsall** | 1-3 | *Brown* |
| | 14 | **H Rushden & D** | 4-1 | *Bertram 2, Brown, Warmer* |
| | 20 | **H Kidderminster** | 3-1 | *Brown 2, Clarke* |
| *Jan* | 18 | A Peterborough | 0-3 | — |

## Youth Alliance Southern League Division One

| | | | | |
|---|---|---|---|---|
| *Jan* | 25 | **H Northampton T** | 0-1 | — |
| *Mar* | 8 | A Peterborough U | 2-2 | *Bertram, Brown* |
| | 15 | A Wycome W | 2-1 | *Bertram, Patterson* |
| | 29 | **H Swindon T** | 1-0 | *Bertram* |
| | 22 | A Cardiff City | 2-2 | *Bertram, Patterson* |
| *Apr* | 4 | A Plymouth A | 2-4 | *Cudworth, Patterson* |
| | 12 | A Portsmouth | 2-0 | *Brown, Smikle* |
| | 19 | **H Bristol R** | 1-1 | *Midworth* |
| | 24 | **H Brentford** | 1-1 | *Midworth* |

## Midland Youth Cup

| | | | | |
|---|---|---|---|---|
| *Oct* | 3 | *****H Burton Albion** | 1-2 | *Warmer* |

\* *Played at The Hawthorns*

## Football League Youth Alliance Cup

| | | | | |
|---|---|---|---|---|
| *Sep* | 7 | **H Shrewsbury** | 0-1 | — |
| | 14 | A Walsall | 1-3 | *Clarke* |
| | 21 | **H Port Vale** | 1-3 | *Warmer* |

## FA Youth Cup

| | | | | |
|---|---|---|---|---|
| *Dec* | 4 | A Millwall | 0-2 | — |

# YOUTHS 2002-03

## Midland Floodlit Youth League

| | | | | | |
|---|---|---|---|---|---|
| Aug | 28 | A Hinckley | 0-1 | — | |
| Sep | 4 | **H Burton Albion** | 2-1 | *Patterson, Sherwood* |
| | 25 | A Kidderminster H | 5-0 | *Elvins 2, Cudworth, Patterson, Sherwood* |
| Oct | 9 | **H Bedworth U** | 2-1 | *McHugh, Holmes* |
| | 23 | **H Boldmere SM** | 5-0 | *Cudworth 2, Clarke, McHugh, Smikle* |
| Nov | 6 | A A Walsall | 0-3 | — |
| | 13 | A Rugby U | 3-0 | *Elvins, Cudworth, Attewell* |
| Dec | 16 | **H Kidderminster** | 3-1 | |
| Jan | 13 | **H Bedworth U** | 11-1 | *Smikle 3, Mbara 2, Cudworth 2, Patterson 2, Elvins, Day* |
| Feb | 24 | A Burton Albion | 1-2 | *Cudworth* |
| Mar | 3 | **H Nuneaton** | 2-0 | *Clarke, Attewell* |
| | 12 | H Quorn | 5-2 | *Smikle, Elvins, Patterson, Hodgkiss, Appleton,* |
| | 19 | **H Hinckley U** | 0-0 | — |
| | 24 | A Nuneaton B | 0-1 | — |
| Apr | 2 | A Boldmere SM | 2-1 | *Hodgkiss 2* |
| | 9 | A Atherstone | 3-1 | *Hodgkiss, Elvins, Barrett* |
| | 23 | **H Atherstone** | 2-1 | *Clarke, Elvins* |
| | 28 | A Quorn | 0-0 | — |
| | 30 | **H Walsall** | 4-2 | *Clarke 2, Cudworth, Martin* |

## Midland Floodlit Youth League Cup [Winners]

| | | | | | |
|---|---|---|---|---|---|
| Oct | 30 | **H Hednesford** | 4-0 | *Clarke, McHugh, Sherwood, Laref* |
| Jan | 15 | A Burton Albion | 4-1 | *Patterson 2, Clarke 2* |
| Feb | 26 | A Coventry Sphinx | 10-0 | *Redshaw 3, Patterson 2, Clarke, Appleton, McHugh* |
| | | | | *Clarkson 2* |
| Mar | 27 | A Marconi | 4-0 | *Patterson, Smikle, Midworth, Clarke* |
| May | 7 | *****H Highate U** | 1-0 | *Sherwood* |

\* *Played at The Hawthorns*

## Staffordshire Junior Cup

| | | | | | |
|---|---|---|---|---|---|
| Oct | 16 | A Chasetown | 10-0 | *Patterson 3, Cudworth 2, Holmes, Clarke, McHugh* |
| | | | | *Smikle, Tomlinson* |
| Nov | 10 | A Stafford Rangers | 2-1 | *Patterson, Smikle* |
| Mar | 10 | A Tamworth | 1-3 | *Patterson* |

**Under-18 side Goals:** *Carey-Bertram 12, Brown 9, Patterson 5, Warmer 3, Smikle 3, Gowling 2,Cudworth 2, Midworth 2, Clarke 2, Attewell 1*

**Under-17 side Goals:** *Patterson 15, Cudworth 10, Sherwood 4, Elvins 7, Clarke 7, Smikle 7, McHugh 4, Holmes 2, Appleton 2, Mbara 2, Attewell 2, Day 1, Hodgkiss 1, Martin 1, Barrett 1, Laref 1, Tomlinson 1*

# YOUTH REVIEW 2003

There was a promotion for the former Youth team coach, Alan Crawford, who was moved up to take charge of the first team. In his place came an old Albion favourite, Craig Shakespeare, who did well in his first season, bringing forward the young players as well as seeing them collect some silverware.

After a good unbeaten start in the Football League Youth Alliance, and with Daniel Carey-Bertram scoring in almost every game, the Under-18 won the Midlands Division, only to fall away in the second half of the season, ending up fifth in the Southern League Division One table, well behind Brentford, who retained the title that they won last year.

There was great disappointment in all the cups. It was a major shock when Burton Albion eliminated holders Albion from the Midland Youth Cup that they had won just six months earlier. All three qualifying games in the Youth Alliance Cup (with its Final at the Millennium Stadium) ended in defeat whilst in the premier competition, Millwall gained revenge for last year with a comfortable 2-0 win at the New Den.

Once again, the Under-17 side were runners-up to Walsall in the MFYL, despite beating their rivals in the last game of the season. They became the first side to win the League Cup for a third time when they beat Highgate United 1-0 in the Hawthorns Final. The Staffordshire Junior Cup — Albion were beaten finalists last year — brought no luck,

*Daniel Carey-Bertram, who played a significant part for the Youth and Reserve sides this season*

despite a 10-0 away win at Coventry Sphinx in the third round; that was the second time during the season that the side hit double figures, following an 11-1 win over Bedworth United.

| Midland Floodlit Youth League | | | | | | |
|---|---|---|---|---|---|---|
| *Premier Division* | | | | | | |
| Walsall | 20 | 16 | 1 | 3 | 56 | 23 | 49 |
| **Albion** | 20 | 14 | 2 | 4 | 50 | 19 | 44 |
| Kiddminster | 20 | 10 | 4 | 6 | 44 | 31 | 34 |
| Nuneaton B | 20 | 10 | 4 | 6 | 34 | 29 | 34 |
| Quorn | 20 | 9 | 5 | 6 | 25 | 27 | 32 |
| Hinckley U | 20 | 7 | 6 | 7 | 19 | 25 | 27 |
| Boldmere SM | 20 | 6 | 4 | 10 | 34 | 37 | 22 |
| Burton A | 20 | 6 | 4 | 10 | 27 | 31 | 22 |
| Bedworth U | 20 | 6 | 3 | 11 | 25 | 44 | 21 |
| Atherstone U | 20 | 4 | 5 | 11 | 17 | 45 | 17 |
| Rugby Utd | 20 | 2 | 2 | 16 | 24 | 44 | 8 |

**Alan Ashman** (1928-2002) will always be remembered as the young 'tracksuit manager' who brought the FA Cup to the Albion in his first season in charge at The Hawthorns. He had inherited a quality set of players from Jimmy Hagan – ironically, Alan's schoolboy footballing idol – but he took them from relegation strugglers in 1967, to Wembley and the FA Cup in 1968.

Always the perfect gentleman in his dealings with players, fans and the press, Alan was shamefully treated in 1971, when he was sacked by the Albion whilst on holiday in Greece, only learning about his fate when a Greek waiter translated the local newspaper for him. The Albion board had gone for the main chance, appointing Don Howe shortly after he had helped coach Arsenal to the Double. It would cost them dearly later on.

Ashman, after a spell managing in Greece, returned to his former club, Carlisle, who he had taken from Division Four to the brink of Division One. By 1974 he had completed the job, pipping Albion for promotion from Division Two, and for a while the Cumbrians were top of the whole Football League. That was also the pinnacle of Alan's career, for he resigned soon afterwards, later becoming assistant manager at Derby, and Chief Scout at a number of clubs.

**Sir Bert Millichip** (1914-2002) was a West Bromwich man who went from being an Albion amateur, to chairman of the club and President of the Football Association, at a time when they exerted their power to split the Football League to form the Premier League.

A member of the Albion board from 1964, and chairman from 1974, he presided over the 'Glory Days' of the late Seventies before moving to the FA in 1984, where he had to cope with Bradford, Heysel and Hillsborough. He was knighted in 1991, and his crowning glory was the success of Euro 1996. His association with the club spanned 66 years.

*Top, Alan Ashman, bottom, Sir Bert Millichip*

Born Ashington November 4 1978 Previous clubs — none. Loan clubs: Mansfield and Halifax

Born Salford December 4 1975 Previous clubs: Manchester United and Preston. Loan clubs: Lincoln and Grimsby

**Albion**

| | League | | Cup | |
|---|---|---|---|---|
| 97-98 | 3 | 0 | 0 | 0 |
| 98-99 | 0 | 0 | 0 | 0 |
| *Mansfield* | | | | |
| 98-99 | 2 | 0 | 0 | 0 |
| **Albion** | | | | |
| 99-00 | 9 | 0 | 1 | 0 |
| *Halifax* | | | | |
| 99-00 | 7 | 0 | 0 | 0 |
| **Albion** | | | | |
| 00-01 | 0 | 0 | 1 | 0 |
| 01-02 | 0 | 0 | 0 | 0 |
| 02-03 | 0 | 0 | 0 | 0 |

Fated never to play a League game under Gary Megson — although he did turn out in the FA Cup tie at Derby County in 2001 — goalkeeper Chris Adamson never recovered from some slack displays in his early games, against Stockport and Sunderland in particular, in 1998. He was only retained last season because of the intervention of chairman Paul Thompson, and left on a 'free' for St Patrick's Athletic early in 2003.

**Manchester United**

| | League | | Cup | |
|---|---|---|---|---|
| 94-95 | 0 | 0 | 0 | 0 |
| *Wimbledon* | | | | |
| 94-95 | 0 | 0 | 3 | 0 |
| *Lincoln City* | | | | |
| 95-96 | 4 | 0 | 0 | 0 |
| **Manchester United** | | | | |
| 95-96 | 0 | 0 | 0 | 0 |
| 96-97 | 0 | 0 | 1+1 | 0 |
| *Grimsby Town* | | | | |
| 96-97 | 10 | 3 | 0 | 0 |
| **Preston NE** | | | | |
| 97-98 | 31+7 | 2 | 8+1 | 1 |
| 98-99 | 13+12 | 2 | 4+1 | 0 |
| 99-00 | 21+5 | 3 | 7 | 1 |
| 00-01 | 25+1 | 5 | 2 | 0 |
| **Albion** | | | | |
| 00-01 | 15 | 0 | 2 | 0 |
| 01-02 | 18 | 0 | 3 | 0 |
| 02-03 | 0 | 0 | 0 | 0 |

Michael's career is still in some doubt after a catastrophic knee injury that he suffered in training in 2002. He went in for a third operation on his knee in March 2003.
Has only played 33 League games in almost three seasons at The Hawthorns since leaving Preston North End.

# IGOR BALIS

Born Czech Republic January 5 1970
Previous club: Spartak Trnava
**Slovakian international**

**Spartak Trnava**

|       | League | Cup |
|-------|--------|-----|
| 95-96 | 32     | 0   |
| 96-97 | 26     | 4   |
| 97-98 | 28     | 0   |
| 98-99 | 26     | 1   |
| 99-00 | 24     | 0   |

**Albion**

| 00-01 | 7    | 0 | 0+1 | 0 |
|-------|------|---|-----|---|
| 01-02 | 32+2 | 2 | 3+1 | 0 |
| 02-03 | 27+1 | 2 | 0+1 | 0 |

There was some concern that Balis' decision to retire from international football would cost the Slovakian full-back his work permit next season, but the player — certainly the coolest and cleverest defender at the club — has been offered a one year extension to his contract subject to Home Office regulations. Unlike many of his colleagues, Igor never looked out of place in the top flight.

# ADAM CHAMBERS

Born Sandwell November 20 1980
Previous club: None **England Youth International**

**Albion**

|       | League | | Cup | |
|-------|--------|---|-----|---|
| 98-99 | 0      | 0 | 0   | 0 |
| 99-00 | 0      | 0 | 0   | 0 |
| 00-01 | 4+7    | 1 | 1+2 | 0 |
| 01-02 | 24+8   | 0 | 7   | 0 |
| 02-03 | 10+3   | 0 | 1+1 | 0 |

Like his brother, Adam found that his Premiership season was disrupted by injury; he will find the Nationwide more suited to his style of play.

# JAMES CHAMBERS

Born Sandwell
November 20
1980
Previous club:
None **England
Youth Interna-
tional**

**Albion**

|  | League |  | Cup |  |
|---|---|---|---|---|
| 98-99 | 0 | 0 | 0 | 0 |
| 99-00 | 10+2 | 0 | 0 | 0 |
| 00-01 | 27+4 | 0 | 5 | 0 |
| 01-02 | 1+4 | 0 | 0+1 | 0 |
| 02-03 | 2+6 | 0 | 1 | 0 |

James Chambers only managed
three starts in an injury-hit season, after missing out badly in
the Division One promotion
campaign the year before.
However, two of those games
were in the final two fixtures,
against Blackburn and Newcastle, when he gave what were
probably the two best performances of his career. No
Albion manager has been
happy playing both twins —
who are very similar in playing
style — in the same team, but,
at the moment, it seems that
James is in the ascendancy, as
he was back in 2000.

# NEIL CLEMENT

Born Reading
October 3 1978
Previous club:
Chelsea Loan
clubs: Reading,
Preston and
Brentford

**Chelsea**

|  | League |  | Cup |  |
|---|---|---|---|---|
| 95-96 | 0 | 0 | 0 | 0 |
| 96-97 | 1 | 0 | 0 | 0 |
| 97-98 | 0 | 0 | 0 | 0 |
| 98-99 | 0 | 0 | 0+2 | 0 |
| *Reading* | | | | |
| 98-99 | 11 | 1 | 0 | 0 |
| *Preston* | | | | |
| 98-99 | 4 | 0 | 0 | 0 |
| **Chelsea** | | | | |
| 99-00 | 0 | 0 | 0 | 0 |
| *Reading* | | | | |
| 99-00 | 7+1 | 0 | 0 | 0 |
| *Albion* | | | | |
| 99-00 | 7+1 | 0 | 0 | 0 |
| **Albion** | | | | |
| 00-01 | 45 | 5 | 7 | 2 |
| 01-02 | 45 | 6 | 7 | 2 |
| 02-03 | 34+2(3) |  | 2+1 | 0 |

Neil was a great disappointment in the Premiership. Not
only did he seem to lose all
confidence gained as an outstanding player in Division
One, he also lost his scoring
touch from free kicks, a knack
that had brought him fifteen
goals in the previous two seasons.

# DANIEL DICHIO

Born Hammersmith October 19 1974
Previous clubs: QPR, Sampdoria, Lecce & Sunderland Loan club: Barnet

## QPR

| | League | | Cup | |
|---|---|---|---|---|
| 93-94 | 0 | 0 | 0 | 0 |

## Barnet

| | | | | |
|---|---|---|---|---|
| 93-94 | 9 | 2 | 0 | 0 |

## QPR

| | | | | |
|---|---|---|---|---|
| 94-95 | 4+5 | 3 | 2 | 0 |
| 95-96 | 21+8 | 10 | 3+1 | 1 |
| 96-97 | 31+6 | 7 | 4+2 | 1 |

## Sampdoria

| | | | | |
|---|---|---|---|---|
| 97-98 | 0 | 0 | | |

## Lecce

| | | | | |
|---|---|---|---|---|
| 97-98 | 4 | 1 | | |

## Sunderland

| | | | | |
|---|---|---|---|---|
| 97-98 | 2+11 | 0 | 0 | 0 |
| 98-99 | 16+20 | 10 | 5+2 | 2 |
| 99-00 | 0+12 | 0 | 3 | 4 |
| 00-01 | 2+13 | 1 | 6+2 | 1 |
| 01-02 | 0 | 0 | 0 | 0 |

## Albion

| | | | | |
|---|---|---|---|---|
| 01-02 | 26+1 | 9 | 4 | 1 |
| 02-03 | 19+9 | 5 | 3 | 3 |

Dichio ended as top scorer in League and Cup, but never really convinced, and ended the season demanding an extension to his contract to make it worthwhile moving his family up from Surrey to live nearer West Bromwich.

# SCOTT DOBIE

Born Workington October 10 1978
Previous club: Carlisle Loan club: Clydebank **Scottish international**

## Carlisle

| | League | | Cup | |
|---|---|---|---|---|
| 96-97 | 0+2 | 1 | 0 | 0 |
| 97-98 | 9+14 | 0 | 1+6 | 0 |
| 98-99 | 26+7 | 6 | 3+1 | 0 |

## Clydebank

| | | | | |
|---|---|---|---|---|
| 98-99 | 6 | 0 | 0 | 0 |

## Carlisle

| | | | | |
|---|---|---|---|---|
| 99-00 | 25+9 | 7 | 4 | 0 |
| 00-01 | 41+3 | 10 | 4+1 | 2 |

## Albion

| | | | | |
|---|---|---|---|---|
| 01-02 | 32+11 | 10 | 4+3 | 2 |
| 02-03 | 10+20 | 5 | 0+3 | 0 |

Scott Dobie's meteoric rise — from the bottom club in the League, to the Premiership and the Scottish national side — was halted when he failed to get regularly into Albion's side. He still ended up as the club's joint top League scorer, scoring two of the best goals of the season,  but lost his place with Scotland.

# LLOYD DYER

Born Birmingham September 13 1982
Previous club: None

**Albion**

02-03    0    0    1    0

Lloyd Dyer will be a mystery to most Albion fans, as his only competitive outing so far was in the disastrous Worthington Cup defeat at Wigan. He was probably the best performer of a pretty bad bunch on the night. Has terrific pace, but there has to be a question mark about his footballing brain at times.

# PHIL GILCHRIST

Born Stockton August 25 1973
Previous clubs: Nottinghm Forest, Middlesbrough, Hartlepool, Oxford & Leicester City

**Nottingham Forest**

|  | League | | Cup | |
|---|---|---|---|---|
| 90-91 | 0 | 0 | 0 | 0 |

**Middlesbrough**

| 91-92 | 0 | 0 | 0 | 0 |
|---|---|---|---|---|

**Hartlepool**

| 92-93 | 24 | 0 | 4 | 0 |
|---|---|---|---|---|
| 93-94 | 30+5 | 0 | 2+1 | 0 |
| 94-95 | 23 | 9 | 7 | 0 |

**Oxford United**

| 94-95 | 18 | 1 | 0 | 0 |
|---|---|---|---|---|
| 95-96 | 42 | 3 | 10 | 0 |
| 96-97 | 38 | 2 | 6 | 0 |
| 97-98 | 35+4 | 2 | 6 | 0 |
| 98-99 | 39 | 2 | 4 | 1 |
| 99-00 | 1 | 0 | 0 | 0 |

**Leicester City**

| 99-00 | 17+10 | 1 | 8+1 | 0 |
|---|---|---|---|---|
| 00-01 | 6+6 | 0 | 2+1 | 0 |

**Albion**

| 00-01 | 8 | 0 | 2 | 0 |
|---|---|---|---|---|
| 01-02 | 43 | 0 | 7 | 0 |
| 02-03 | 22 | 0 | 1+1 | 0 |

Another solid season for the defender, albeit another one full of injury, this time causing him to miss a good half of the season. Another player who will shine in Division One.

# SEAN GREGAN | # RUSSELL HOULT

Born Stockton
March 29 1974
Previous
clubs: Darling-
ton & Preston

Born Ashby
November 22
1972
Previous clubs:
Leicester, Derby
& Portsmouth
Loan clubs: Lin-
coln, Blackpool,
Bolton & Derby

## Darlington

|       | League | | Cup | |
|-------|--------|---|------|---|
| 91-92 | 17    | 0 | 2    | 0 |
| 92-93 | 15+2  | 1 | 2    | 0 |
| 93-94 | 21+2  | 1 | 4    | 0 |
| 94-95 | 22+3  | 2 | 4+1  | 0 |
| 95-96 | 38    | 0 | 0    | 0 |
| 96-97 | 16    | 0 | 4    | 0 |

## Preston NE

|       | League | | Cup | |
|-------|--------|---|------|---|
| 96-97 | 21    | 1 | 0    | 0 |
| 97-98 | 33+2  | 2 | 9    | 2 |
| 98-99 | 40+1  | 3 | 5    | 0 |
| 99-00 | 33    | 3 | 10   | 0 |
| 00-01 | 39+2  | 2 | 3    | 0 |
| 01-02 | 40+1  | 1 | 4    | 9 |

## Albion

|       | League | | Cup | |
|-------|--------|---|------|---|
| 02-03 | 36    | 1 | 2    | 0 |

One of Albion's big-money signings at the start of the season, he arrived late, but soon settled down to play an important part in the side. However, he always looked better when he played in midfield, rather than at the back, where he played most of his games. Makes too many errors for a defender in the Premiership, but will be more at home back in Division One.

## Leicester City

|       | League | | Cup | |
|-------|--------|---|------|---|
| 90-91 | 0     | 0 | 0    | 0 |
| 91-92 | 0     | 0 | 0    | 0 |

## Lincoln City

|       | League | | Cup | |
|-------|--------|---|------|---|
| 91-92 | 2     | 0 | 0    | 0 |

## Blackpool

|       | League | | Cup | |
|-------|--------|---|------|---|
| 91-92 | 0     | 0 | 0    | 0 |

## Leicester City

|       | League | | Cup | |
|-------|--------|---|------|---|
| 92-93 | 10    | 0 | 4    | 0 |
| 93-94 | 0     | 0 | 0    | 0 |

## Bolton W

|       | League | | Cup | |
|-------|--------|---|------|---|
| 93-94 | 3+1   | 0 | 0    | 0 |

## Leicester City

|       | League | | Cup | |
|-------|--------|---|------|---|
| 94-95 | 0     | 0 | 0    | 0 |

## Lincoln City

|       | League | | Cup | |
|-------|--------|---|------|---|
| 94-95 | 15    | 0 | 1    | 9 |

## Derby County

|       | League | | Cup | |
|-------|--------|---|------|---|
| 94-95 | 15    | 0 | 0    | 0 |
| 95-96 | 40+1  | 0 | 3    | 0 |
| 96-97 | 31+1  | 0 | 5    | 0 |
| 97-98 | 2     | 0 | 1    | 0 |
| 98-99 | 23    | 0 | 3    | 0 |
| 99-00 | 10    | 0 | 3    | 0 |

## Portsmouth

|       | League | | Cup | |
|-------|--------|---|------|---|
| 99-00 | 18    | 0 | 4    | 0 |
| 00-01 | 22    | 0 | 4    | 0 |

## Albion

|       | League | | Cup | |
|-------|--------|---|------|---|
| 00-01 | 13    | 0 | 2    | 0 |
| 01-02 | 45    | 0 | 7    | 0 |
| 02-03 | 37    | 0 | 2    | 0 |

## LEE HUGHES

Born Smethwick May 22 1976
Previous clubs: Kidderminster Harriers & Coventry City

**Albion**

|  | League | | Cup | |
|---|---|---|---|---|
| 97-98 | 18+19 | 14 | 2+2 | 0 |
| 98-99 | 42 | 31 | 3 | 1 |
| 99-00 | 36 | 12 | 7 | 1 |
| 00-01 | 41 | 21 | 6+1 | 2 |
| **Coventry City** | | | | |
| 01-02 | 35+3 | 14 | 1+1 | 0 |
| **Albion** | | | | |
| 02-03 | 14+9 | 0 | 1 | 1 |

After a stunning early record with the club, when he scored once every two games, Hughes left for Coventry for a record £5m. After a season there, where he still ended as top scorer, he returned to the Albion for £2.5m, in a blaze of publicity two weeks into the season — and flopped disastrously. He failed to score at all in the Premiership — supporting the theory that he was purely a Nationwide player — and recorded his only goal against Wigan. Next season will surely be one of reckoning for Hughesie; will he regain his lost scoring touch?

## BRIAN JENSEN

Born Copenhagen June 8 1975
Previous club: AZ Alkmaar

**AZ Alkmaar**

|  | League | | Cup | |
|---|---|---|---|---|
| 97-98 | 0 | 0 | | |
| 98-99 | 1 | 0 | | |
| **Albion** | | | | |
| 99-00 | 12 | 0 | 0 | 0 |
| 00-01 | 33 | 0 | 4 | 0 |
| 01-02 | 1 | 0 | 1 | 0 |
| 02-03 | 0 | 0 | 0 | 0 |

RELEASED

Goalkeeper Brian Jensen — The Beast — was released at the end of the season, after playing just one League game in nearly three years. The signing of Joe Murphy meant that the Great Dane had dropped to number three in the goalkeeping ranking, and a frank interview he gave to a Danish newspaper during the season did him no favours. Always a favourite with the fans, despite a tendency to stay rooted to his line.

# ANDY JOHNSON

Born Bristol May 2 1974 Previous clubs: Norwich & Nottingham Forest **Welsh international**

## Norwich City

|  | League | | Cup | |
|---|---|---|---|---|
| 91-92 | 2 | 0 | 0 | 0 |
| 92-93 | 1+1 | 1 | 0 | 0 |
| 93-94 | 0+2 | 0 | 1 | 0 |
| 94-95 | 6+1 | 0 | 0 | 0 |
| 95-96 | 23+3 | 7 | 3+1 | 1 |
| 96-97 | 24+3 | 5 | 2 | 1 |

## Nottingham Forest

|  | League | | Cup | |
|---|---|---|---|---|
| 97-98 | 24+10 | 4 | 2+1 | 0 |
| 98-99 | 25+3 | 0 | 3 | 1 |
| 99-00 | 24+1 | 2 | 0 | 0 |
| 00-01 | 29+2 | 3 | 1 | 0 |
| 01-02 | 1 | 0 | 0 | 0 |

## Albion

|  | League | | Cup | |
|---|---|---|---|---|
| 01-02 | 28+4 | 4 | 4 | 1 |
| 02-03 | 30+2 | 1 | 2 | 0 |

After playing a key part in the promotion season, Johnson failed to impress in the Premiership, despite his experience there with Norwich and Forest. Sidelined by suspension and then injury, after he broke his foot, he will be expected to make a greater contribution in the coming season.

# JORDAO

Born Malanje, Angola August 30 1971 Previous clubs: Amadora, Leca, Campomaiorense, Benfica & Braga

## Amadora

|  | League | | Cup | |
|---|---|---|---|---|
| 90-91 | 0 | 0 | | |
| 91-92 | 17 | 3 | | |
| 92-93 | 3 | 0 | | |

## Campomaiorense

|  | League | | Cup | |
|---|---|---|---|---|
| 93-94 | 9 | 0 | | |

## Leca

|  | League | | Cup | |
|---|---|---|---|---|
| 94-95 | 26 | 3 | | |

## Amadora

|  | League | | Cup | |
|---|---|---|---|---|
| 95-96 | 30 | 1 | | |
| 96-97 | 31 | 3 | | |

## Benfica

|  | League | | Cup | |
|---|---|---|---|---|
| 97-98 | 6 | 0 | | |

## Braga

|  | League | | Cup | |
|---|---|---|---|---|
| 97-98 | 14 | 1 | | |
| 9899 | 29 | 1 | | |
| 99-00 | 22 | 0 | | |

## Albion

|  | League | | Cup | |
|---|---|---|---|---|
| 00-01 | 35 | 1 | 4+2 | 1 |
| 01-02 | 19+6 | 5 | 0+1 | 1 |
| 02-03 | 0+3 | 0 | 1 | 0 |

An unfortunate season for the Angola-born Portuguese midfielder; shunned by his manager for most of the season, he tore his Achilles tendon in an end of season reserve game, just a few days before being officially released by the club.

## JASON KOUMAS

Born Wrexham September 25 1979
Previous club: Tranmere Rovers
**Welsh international**

**Tranmere Rovers**

|       | League |    | Cup |   |
|-------|--------|----|-----|---|
| 97-98 | 0      | 0  | 0   | 0 |
| 98-99 | 11+12  | 3  | 3+1 | 1 |
| 99-00 | 9+14   | 2  | 3+3 | 0 |
| 00-01 | 34+5   | 10 | 7+1 | 1 |
| 01-02 | 38     | 8  | 5   | 5 |

**Albion**

|       | League |   | Cup |   |
|-------|--------|---|-----|---|
| 02-03 | 27+5   | 4 | 3   | 0 |

Without question, Jason Koumas was the one outstanding find of the season for the Albion. After protracted negotiations had broken down the previous season, the Welsh Under-21 international was signed for a record £2m deal from Tranmere two weeks into the Premiership campaign. Megson's insistence on keeping him on the bench for the early part of his time at the club meant that it was some time before he began to shine, but he ended the season's as Albion's one true class performer, as well as a full Welsh international in Mark Hughes' successful side.

## DES LYTTLE

Born Wolverhampton September 24 1971
Previous clubs: Swansea, Nottingham Forest & Watford.
Loan club: Port Vale

**Swansea City**

|       | League |   | Cup |   |
|-------|--------|---|-----|---|
| 92-93 | 46     | 1 |     |   |

**Nottingham Forest**

|       | League |   | Cup |   |
|-------|--------|---|-----|---|
| 93-94 | 37     | 1 |     |   |
| 94-95 | 38     | 0 | 6   | 0 |
| 95-96 | 32+1   | 1 | 15  | 0 |
| 96-97 | 30+2   | 1 | 5   | 0 |
| 97-98 | 35     | 0 | 5   | 0 |
| 98-99 | 5+5    | 0 | 2+1 | 0 |

*Port Vale*

|       | League |   | Cup |   |
|-------|--------|---|-----|---|
| 98-99 | 7      | 0 | 0   | 0 |

**Watford**

|       | League |   | Cup |   |
|-------|--------|---|-----|---|
| 99-00 | 11     | 0 | 1   | 0 |

**Albion**

|       | League |   | Cup |   |
|-------|--------|---|-----|---|
| 99-00 | 8+1    | 0 | 0   | 0 |
| 00-01 | 38+2   | 1 | 7   | 0 |
| 01-02 | 13+10  | 0 | 4+1 | 0 |
| 02-03 | 2+2    | 0 | 1   | 0 |

Another player harshly treated by Megson, but when called up out of necessity for the last few games, gave some excellent performances that indicate he still has a few games left in him — but not at West Bromwich Albion.

## LEE MARSHALL

Born Islington January 21 1979 Previous clubs: Norwich & Leicester City

### Norwich City

|        | League | | Cup | |
|--------|--------|---|-----|---|
| 96-97  | 0      | 0 | 0   | 0 |
| 97-98  | 2+2    | 0 | 0   | 0 |
| 98-99  | 38+6   | 3 | 6   | 0 |
| 99-00  | 21+12  | 5 | 2+1 | 1 |
| 00-01  | 34+2   | 3 |     |   |

### Leicester City

|        | League | |
|--------|--------|---|
| 00-01  | 7+2    | 0 |
| 01-02  | 29+6   | 0 |

### Albion

|        |        | | | |
|--------|--------|---|---|---|
| 02-03  | 4+5(1) | | 1 | 0 |

It is difficult for Albion fans to have got any great impression of Lee Marshall, for not long after signing from Leicester City for £750,000, he fell foul of Gary Megson, and spent most of the season as the highest-paid Reserve player in Albion's history. Transfer-listed at the end of the season, he did at least manage to score Albion's first-ever goal in the Premiership, at home to Leeds.

## DEREK McINNES

Born Paisley July 6 1971 Previous clubs: Morton, Rangers & Toulouse Loan club: Stockport County

**Scottish international**

### Greenock Morton

|        | League | | Cup | |
|--------|--------|---|-----|---|
| 87-88  | 1+1    | 0 |     |   |
| 88-89  | 24+5   | 1 |     |   |
| 89-90  | 15+8   | 1 |     |   |
| 90-91  | 24+7   | 3 |     |   |
| 91-92  | 38+4   | 7 |     |   |
| 92-93  | 40     | 2 |     |   |
| 93-94  | 16     | 1 |     |   |
| 94-95  | 26     | 3 | 3   | 0 |
| 95-96  | 12     | 1 |     |   |

### Rangers

|        | League | | Cup | |
|--------|--------|---|-----|---|
| 95-96  | 5+1    | 0 | 0   | 0 |
| 96-97  | 10+11  | 1 | 7+5 | 3 |
| 97-98  | 0      | 0 | 0   | 0 |
| 98-99  | 0+7    | 0 | 0   | 0 |

### *Stockport County*

|        |    | | | |
|--------|----|---|---|---|
| 98-99  | 13 | 0 | 1 | 0 |

### Toulouse

|        |   | | | |
|--------|---|---|---|---|
| 99-00  | 3 | 0 | 0 | 0 |

### Albion

|        |      | | | |
|--------|------|---|---|---|
| 00-01  | 14   | 1 | 4 | 0 |
| 01-02  | 45   | 3 | 7 | 0 |
| 02-03  | 28+1 | 2 | 1 | 0 |

Not a great season for the inspirational captain, but he did, deservedly, secure caps for Berti Vogts' Scotland side.

## DARREN MOORE

Born Handsworth April 22 1974 Previous clubs: Torquay, Doncaster, Bradford City & Portsmouth **Jamaican international**

**Torquay United**

| | League | | Cup | |
|---|---|---|---|---|
| 91-92 | 5 | 1 | 0 | 0 |
| 92-93 | 30+1 | 2 | 6 | 0 |
| 93-94 | 37 | 2 | 5 | 1 |
| 94-95 | 30 | 3 | 8 | 1 |

**Doncaster Rovers**

| | | | | |
|---|---|---|---|---|
| 95-96 | 35 | 2 | 4 | 1 |
| 96-97 | 41 | 5 | 3 | 0 |

**Bradford City**

| | | | | |
|---|---|---|---|---|
| 97-98 | 18 | 0 | 0 | 0 |
| 98-99 | 44 | 3 | 7 | 1 |
| 99-00 | 0 | 0 | 0 | 0 |

**Portsmouth**

| | | | | |
|---|---|---|---|---|
| 99-00 | 25 | 1 | 1 | 0 |
| 00-01 | 31+1 | 1 | 5 | 0 |
| 01-02 | 2 | 0 | 1 | 0 |

**Albion**

| | | | | |
|---|---|---|---|---|
| 01-02 | 31+1 | 2 | 4 | 0 |
| 02-03 | 29 | 2 | 2 | 0 |

The man whose goal against Crystal Palace ensured Premiership football saw his season curtailed prematurely with a serious knee injury against Chelsea. A good, solid First Division player who was caught out a number of times at the highest level.

## JOE MURPHY

Born Dublin August 21 1981 Previous club:Tranmere Rovers **Irish Under-21 international**

**Tranmere Rovers**

| | League | | Cup | |
|---|---|---|---|---|
| 99-00 | 21 | 0 | 6 | 0 |
| 00-01 | 19+1 | 0 | 1 | 0 |
| 01-02 | 21+1 | 0 | 5 | 0 |
| **Albion** | | | | |
| 02-03 | 1+1 | 0 | 1 | 0 |

It is hard to imagine a better start for a club than the one which fell to young Joe Murphy, when he saved a penalty from England's Michael Owen, in front of his whole Liverpool-supporting family, at Anfield. Incredibly, the save was his first touch of the ball in an Albion shirt, after coming on as a substitute for the dismissed Russell Hoult.

Although Murphy only played twice more, he established himself as second choice keeper ahead of Brian Jensen, and was named as the Republic of Ireland's *Under-21 Player of The Year*. Should have a great future at the club.

# JASON ROBERTS

Born Park
Royal January
25 1978
Previous clubs:
Wolves & Bristol Rovers
Loan clubs:
Torquay &
Bristol City

**Grenadian international**

## Wolves

| | League | | Cup | |
|---|---|---|---|---|
| 97-98 | 0 | 0 | 0 | 0 |

*Torquay United*

| | | | | |
|---|---|---|---|---|
| 97-98 | 13+1 | 6 | 0 | 0 |

*Bristol City*

| | | | | |
|---|---|---|---|---|
| 97-98 | 1+2 | 1 | 0 | 0 |

**Bristol Rovers**

| | | | | |
|---|---|---|---|---|
| 98-99 | 32+5 | 16 | 8 | 7 |
| 99-00 | 41 | 22 | 7 | 3 |

**Albion**

| | | | | |
|---|---|---|---|---|
| 00-01 | 32+11 | 14 | 6+1 | 3 |
| 01-02 | 12+2 | 7 | 3 | 0 |
| 02-03 | 31+1 | 3 | 2 | 0 |

The greatest disappointment of the Premiership season, for Cyrille Regis' nephew was expected to revel in the extra space and time afforded to players in the top flight. After a good start, his season faded away, and he ended up with more bookings that goals. He was singled out by defenders — and won more free kicks than any other player in the Premiership — but his attitude won few friends.

# LARUS SIGURDSSON

Born Akureyri,
Iceland June 4
1973
Previous club:
Stoke City
**Icelandic
international**

## Stoke City

| | League | | Cup | |
|---|---|---|---|---|
| 94-95 | 22+1 | 1 | 0 | 0 |
| 95-96 | 46 | 0 | 9 | 0 |
| 96-97 | 45 | 0 | 5 | 0 |
| 97-98 | 43 | 1 | 6 | 0 |
| 98-99 | 38 | 4 | 5 | 0 |
| 99-00 | 5 | 1 | 2 | 0 |

**Albion**

| | | | | |
|---|---|---|---|---|
| 99-00 | 27 | 0 | 1 | 0 |
| 00-01 | 7+5 | 0 | 0+1 | 0 |
| 01-02 | 42+1 | 1 | 7 | 0 |
| 02-03 | 23+6 | 0 | 2+1 | 0 |

The tough, no-nonsense Icelander has got over serious injury (in 2000) and being sold once by Gary Megson (at Stoke in 1999) to earn an almost guaranteed place in the Albion defence, as well as that of his country. Although somewhat out of his depth at the highest level, he will be expected to shine in Division One during 2003-04.

## BOB TAYLOR

Born Easington February 3 1967 Previous clubs: Leeds, Bristol City & Bolton Loan club: Bolton

**Leeds United**

| | League | | Cup | |
|---|---|---|---|---|
| 85-86 | 2 | 0 | 0 | 0 |
| 86-87 | 2 | 0 | 3+1 | 1 |
| 87-88 | 27+5 | 9 | 7 | 3 |
| 88-89 | 2+4 | 0 | 0+1 | 0 |

**Bristol City**

| | | | | |
|---|---|---|---|---|
| 88-89 | 12 | 8 | 0 | 0 |
| 89-90 | 37 | 27 | 10 | 8 |
| 90-91 | 34+5 | 11 | 6 | 0 |
| 91-92 | 13+5 | 4 | 2+1 | 1 |

**Albion**

| | | | | |
|---|---|---|---|---|
| 91-92 | 17 | 8 | 0 | 0 |
| 92-93 | 46 | 30 | 13 | 7 |
| 93-94 | 42 | 18 | 9+1 | 3 |
| 94-95 | 38+4 | 11 | 1+1 | 0 |
| 95-96 | 39+3 | 17 | 10+2 | 6 |
| 96-97 | 16+16 | 10 | 2+1 | 0 |
| 97-98 | 11+4 | 2 | 3 | 1 |

*Bolton Wanderers*

| | | | | |
|---|---|---|---|---|
| 97-98 | 10+2 | 3 | 0 | 0 |

**Bolton Wanderers**

| | | | | |
|---|---|---|---|---|
| 98-99 | 32+6 | 15 | 7+3 | 3 |
| 99-00 | 15+12 | 3 | 6+3 | 3 |

**Albion**

| | | | | |
|---|---|---|---|---|
| 90-00 | 8 | 5 | 0 | 0 |
| 00-01 | 17+23 | 5 | 2+4 | 1 |
| 01-02 | 18+16 | 7 | 3+1 | 0 |
| 02-03 | 2+2 | 0 | 0 | 0 |

Bob's Testimonial season was a sad one, with only two starts

## IFEANYI UDEZE

Born Lagos July 21 1980 Previous clubs: Insurance (Nigeria), Kavala (Greece) PAOK Salonika **Nigerian international**

**Insurance**

| | League | | Cup |
|---|---|---|---|
| 97-98 | 12 | 0 | |

**Kavala**

| | | | |
|---|---|---|---|
| 97-98 | 21+1 | 0 | |
| 98-99 | 12+2 | 0 | |
| 99-00 | 23 | 0 | |

**PAOK Salonika**

| | | | |
|---|---|---|---|
| 00-01 | 16 | 0 | |
| 01-02 | 14 | 0 | |
| 02-03 | 3 | 0 | |

**Albion**

| | | | | |
|---|---|---|---|---|
| 02-03 | 7+4 | 0 | 0 | 0 |

The Nigerian international full-back, who started his career with Insurance, of Nigeria, before moving on to Greece (where his side won the Greek Cup in 2001), and fame in the 2002 World Cup (where he was his country's best performer against England) was brought in on loan during January's transfer window. He always looked out of place, and it speaks volumes that he failed to displace the out-of-form Clement. Released at the end of the season, to return to PAOK.

## RONNIE WALLWORK

Born Manchester September 10 1977 Previous club: Manchester United Loan clubs: Carlisle & Stockport

**Manchester United**

| | | | |
|---|---|---|---|
| 94-95 | 0 | 0 | 0 | 0 |
| 95-96 | 0 | 0 | 0 | 0 |
| 96-97 | 0 | 0 | 0 | 0 |
| 97-98 | 0 | 0 | 0+1 | 0 |

*Carlisle United*

| | | | |
|---|---|---|---|
| 97-98 | 10 | 1 | 0 | 0 |

*Stockport County*

| | | | |
|---|---|---|---|
| 97-98 | 7 | 0 | 0 | 0 |

**Manchester United**

| | | | |
|---|---|---|---|
| 98-99 | 0 | 0 | 0+1 | 0 |
| 99-00 | 0+5 | 0 | 1 | 0 |
| 00-01 | 4+8 | 0 | 2+2 | 0 |
| 01-02 | 0 | 0 | 2 | 0 |

**Albion**

| | | | |
|---|---|---|---|
| 02-03 | 23+4 | 0 | 3 | 0 |

Wallwork was described as "The best Bosman signing in the Premiership" by his then manager Sir Alex Ferguson — but then he would say that, wouldn't he? The owner of a Premiership winners' medal from 2001, the player was a great disappointment in Albion's midfield during the season. It remains to be seen whether he can stamp some sort of authority on games in the Nationwide League.

# International Honours 2002-03

Six Albion players were selected for their countries in full internationals during the 2002-03 season; two for Scotland, two for Wales, and one each for Iceland and Nigeria. Joe Murphy represented the Republic of Ireland at Under-21 level, and was named Irish Under-21 Player of the Year.

On an unofficial level, both Jason Roberts and Darren Moore played for a Rest of the World side against an African XI in a charity match at the Reebok Stadium.

**Scott Dobie** (Scotland) v. *Denmark* 21.8.02 (sub), v. *Faroes* 7.9.02 (EC), v. *Portugal* 20.11.02

**Derek McInnes** (Scotland) v. *Denmark* 21.8.02 (sub) v. *Portugal* 20.11.02 (sub)

**Larus Sigurdsson** (Iceland) v. *Hungary* 8.9.02, v. *Scotland* 12.10.02 (EC), v. *Scotland* 29.3.03 (EC), v. *Finland* 30.4.03 v. *Faroes* 7.6.03, v. *Lithuania* 11.6.03

**Andy Johnson** (Wales) *Croatia* 21.8.03, *Finland* 7.9.02 (EC), *USA* 26.5.03

**Jason Koumas** (Wales) v. *Bosnia & Herzegovina* 12.2.03 (sub) *USA* 26.5.03

**Ifeanyi Udeze** (Nigeria) v. *Malawi* 29.3.03 (ANC)

**Joe Murphy** (Republic of Ireland) U-21 v *Finland* 20.8.02, U-21 v. *Russia* 7.9.02, U-21 v. *Switzerland* 15.10.02

# FANS' ROLLCALL

| | | |
|---|---|---|
| 001 John Homer | 075 John Houghton | 149 Adam Gregson |
| 002 Joan Willmore | 076 Peter Knowles | 150 Margaret Gill |
| 003 Valerie Willmore | 077 David Warner | 151 Kirsty Gill |
| 004 Dave Holloway | 078 Janet Bennett | 152 Martyn J Wheeler |
| 005 Vicki Ashfield | 079 Adam Dyke | 153 John Aston |
| 006 Dorothy Ingram | 080 Rory Dyke | 154 Katie Aston |
| 007 Sarah-Jane Homer | 081 John Griffin | 155 Samantha Aston |
| 008 David T Homer | 082 Ann Wooldridge | 146 Peter Thursfield |
| 009 Kevin Grice | 083 Garth Wooldridge | 157 Andrew Holt |
| 010 Daniel Grice | 084 Albert E Davis | 158 Brian Partridge |
| 011 Thomas Grice | 085 Kevin Witten | 159 Richard Bramwell |
| 012 David Hewitt | 086 Julian Rowe | 160 Julian Dowen |
| 013 Garry Wheeler | 087 Richard Brennan | 161 John Burke |
| 014 N G Walker | 088 Reg Snell | 162 K T Poole |
| 015 Steve Waterhouse | 089 M Wilson | 163 Nicola Jayne Tranter |
| 016 Richard Jones | 090 Geoff Allman | 164 Darren Tranter |
| 017 Ray Priest | 091 Barry Brisland | 165 Steve Morris |
| 018 Amanda Palfrey | 092 M Leyland | 166 Sophie Morris |
| 019 Pete Sargent | 093 S A Moss | 167 Ellie Morris |
| 020 Andy Wilce | 094 Alfred A Clark | 168 Eamonn Gallagher |
| 021 Darren Cooper | 095 Karen Wright | 169 Guy Smith |
| 022 Dougie Webb | 096 Terry Wills | 170 Janet Rayner |
| 023 Teresa Fryer | 097 Malcolm Allsopp | 171 Julie Walton |
| 024 Dave Baxendale | 098 Daniel Lewis | 172 Bob The Wulf |
| 025 Peter Baxendale | 099 Aaron Luxton | 173 Wayne Boothroyd |
| 026 Steve Cannon | 100 Oliver Willmore | 174 D C Clarke |
| 027 Ian Tubby | 101 Amy Batham | 175 M Clarke |
| 028 Mark Hitcox | 102 Emily Batham | 176 Tony Messenger |
| 029 Les H Woodhall | 103 Mark W Bifield | 177 Simon Davies |
| 030 Stephen Hyde | 104 Matthew Whitehouse | 178 Terry O'Connell |
| 031 Mark J Whitehouse | 105 Mike Phipps | 179 Andy Tompkins |
| 032 K L Melhuish | 106 Davey Brett | 180 Mike Gale |
| 033 Dave Bunt | 107 Robert L Mills | 181 Andrew Curran |
| 034 Michelle Bennett | 108 Stephen J Mills | 182 F C Simms |
| 035 Stuart Bennett | 109 Richard W Mills | 183 David Miles |
| 036 Mark Bell | 110 Craig Alan Westwood | 184 Andrew Phillips |
| 037 Ian Hoult | 111 D R Sharpe | 185 John Williamson |
| 038 Archie Ryan | 112 Richard Haddlesey | 186 Keith Robert Fisher |
| 039 Dave Walker | 113 Peter J Gregory | 187 Andy Jukes |
| 040 Mark A Whitehouse | 114 David Russell | 188 Paul 'Dozy' Richards |
| 041 Craig A Whitehouse | 115 Chris Marsh | 189 Terry Stanley |
| 042 Adam M Whitehouse | 116 Chris Dawson | 190 Paul Murray |
| 043 Trevor Challoner | 117 D A Billingham | 191 R Slater |
| 044 Jeff Prestridge | 118 Jonathan C Round | 192 Simon Slater |
| 045 David Prestridge | 119 Chris Prinn | 193 David Slater |
| 046 Cathy Maddox | 120 Rob Cunningham | 194 Neil John Slater |
| 047 John Maddox | 121 Spiro Marcetic | 195 Ken Smith |
| 048 Mike Phipps | 122 Martin L James | 196 S Brookes |
| 049 Dean Walton | 123 P S W Jeremy | 197 Brian Walker |
| 050 Robert Aiken | 124 Neil Kirkham | 198 Matthew Whitehouse |
| 051 James Meighan | 125 Brian Kirkham | 199 Michael Griffiths |
| 052 Paul Collins | 126 Mel Turner | 200 Dave Howell |
| 053 David Mills | 127 Simon Wall | 201 Mick Corfield |
| 054 Claire Hunt | 128 Peter Wall | 202 William Corfield |
| 055 Alistair Partridge | 129 Clive Griffin | 203 Brian Cooper |
| 056 Keith R Hill | 130 Helen Moore | 204 Steve Tongue |
| 057 Chris Dawson | 131 Nick Fletcher | 205 Ellie Tongue |
| 058 Gavin Paul | 132 Alan W Lowndes | 206 Paul Bunn |
| 059 Dave Taylor | 133 Moray Allan | 207 Ian Stimpson |
| 060 John A Castle | 134 Alan Davies | 208 Lauren Haywood |
| 061 Michael Thomas | 135 Jamie Burrows | 209 Robert Smith |
| 062 Jeff Burges | 136 Shane Harper | 210 Roy Bradshaw |
| 063 Richard Barton | 137 Dave Tongue | 211 Andy Heselgrove |
| 064 W D Ellis | 138 Philip A Russell | 212 Callum Heselgrove |
| 065 Tony Matthews | 139 David P Russell | 213 Alan Phillips |
| 066 Peter Hall | 140 Cavan Timmins | 214 Roy Wimbury |
| 067 Alan Wheatley | 141 Colin Mackenzie | 215 Paul Millard |
| 068 George Prest | 142 Robert Bradley | 216 Mark T Steventon |
| 069 John Rowe | 143 William Hayward | 217 Gary Marton |
| 070 Paula Beardsmore | 144 Anthony Pick | 218 Nicholas J Hynes |
| 071 Jonathan Want | 145 Tom Priest | 219 Doug Ralley |
| 072 D T Lloyd | 146 T W Basterfield | 220 Lee Matthew Smith |
| 073 Tony Turner | 147 Leonard Gardner | 221 Jayne Gazey |
| 074 Martin Banner | 148 Adam Barker | 222 Rebecca Gazey |

*126*

| | | | | | |
|---|---|---|---|---|---|
| 223 | Steven Lloyd | 301 | Paul Foster | 379 | Ian Wedge |
| 224 | Hazel Hughes | 302 | Richard Ralphs | 380 | David Hands |
| 225 | Jamie Arrowsmith | 303 | Lacey V Bucknall | 381 | Alan Mascall |
| 226 | A M Rogers | 304 | Kev Martin | 382 | David Paul Benton |
| 227 | Roger Matcham | 305 | Helen Martin | 383 | Paul Malcom Burke |
| 228 | John Reade | 306 | Jack Martin | 384 | Allan Maull |
| 229 | Vanessa Vowles | 307 | Steven Alford | 385 | Helen Maull |
| 230 | Bruce Allison | 308 | Tony Green | 386 | Dave Haynes |
| 231 | Robert Higgins | 309 | Lisa Thompson | 387 | Stuart Turnbull |
| 232 | Alan Topping | 310 | Stephen Beech | 388 | Neil Morris |
| 233 | Gerard Small | 311 | Joan Freeman | 389 | Hugh Workman |
| 234 | Martin Chatwin | 312 | Simon Crockett | 390 | Christopher Hall |
| 235 | Garry D Elwell | 313 | Mark Roger Sutton | 391 | Dave Siviter |
| 236 | Robert G Elwell | 314 | Charles Waldock | 392 | Leonard Green |
| 237 | Peter J Elwell | 315 | Michael Lee | 393 | Gary Woodward |
| 238 | Elaine S Elwell | 316 | Simon Saverton | 394 | Michael Andrew Woodward |
| 239 | Samuel R Harris | 317 | Tony Parris | 395 | Andrew Timms |
| 240 | Steve Whitehouse | 318 | Roy Cooper | 396 | Jonathan Eden |
| 241 | P A Wood | 319 | Tony Bray | 397 | Verity Eden |
| 242 | M F Wood | 320 | Alan Beetlestone | 398 | Glora Hiscocks |
| 243 | Ryan Guest | 321 | T Cook (Cookie) | 399 | David Hiscocks |
| 244 | Cliff Price | 322 | D J Metcalfe | 400 | Anthony Brierley |
| 245 | Steve Stokes | 323 | Paul Harrison | 401 | William Henry Broadhouse |
| 246 | Amanda Stokes | 324 | Michael Leslie Tippler | 402 | Anthony Loynes |
| 247 | Clive Smith | 325 | Neil Graham Tipler | 403 | Tina Loynes |
| 248 | K Pegler | 326 | Nik Jones | 404 | Jake Anthony Loynes |
| 249 | Paul Homer | 327 | Lewis Madden | 405 | Joshua John Loynes |
| 250 | R Morris | 328 | Alan Hobson | 406 | Lucy Phipps |
| 251 | Mike Mihailovic | 329 | Darren Gregg | 407 | Barry Phipps |
| 252 | James Keys | 330 | Samuel C Gregg-Lester | 408 | David Davies |
| 253 | Len Bowkett | 331 | Lew Clews | 409 | Steve Mole |
| 254 | Thomas Bunn | 332 | Richard Leatherland | 410 | Luke Cole |
| 255 | R J Toy | 333 | Norman Hathaway | 411 | Stefan Cole |
| 256 | John Barlow | 334 | Stephanie Hickmans | 412 | Lenny 'H' Weston |
| 257 | Kelvin Rzepkowski | 335 | Chris Hickmans | 413 | Rebekah Stringer |
| 258 | Samuel Bradley | 336 | Frank Hope | 414 | Maria Forster |
| 259 | M K Taylor | 337 | Marguerite Bibb | 415 | Lance Forster |
| 260 | Alan Jarvis | 338 | Anne Bibb | 416 | Steve Finn |
| 261 | Lee Corcoran | 339 | Jane Bibb | 417 | Linda Millard |
| 262 | Kevin Daw | 340 | Anthony J Curtis | 418 | C T Jones |
| 263 | Thomas Daw | 341 | Andy Bosworth | 419 | J Donovan |
| 264 | Stephen D Dunn | 342 | Rob Bishop | 420 | Joseph Donovan Jnr |
| 265 | Harold Pearson | 343 | John Monkton | 421 | Helen Donovan |
| 266 | Nikki Timmis | 344 | Ted Elnor | 422 | Michelle Lyons |
| 267 | S D Antis | 345 | Hitesh Patel | 423 | Louis Wall |
| 268 | Ian Woods | 346 | Dave Dyer | 424 | Christine Wall |
| 269 | Jamie Woods | 347 | Hilary Boddy | 425 | Bill Clee |
| 270 | Lee Ball | 348 | John Whitton | 426 | The Farrington Family |
| 271 | Daniel Green | 349 | K P Siggins | 427 | Andrew John Grove |
| 272 | Oliver Green | 350 | H G Siggins | 428 | Nicholas Ball |
| 273 | Keith Wheeler | 351 | Leonard Shuker | 429 | Bill Young |
| 274 | David Grant | 352 | David J Watkin | 430 | Olivia Young |
| 275 | Peter A Grant | 353 | Robert Hinsley | 431 | Robert Young |
| 276 | John Sutton | 354 | Stephen Hinsley | 432 | J L R Walker |
| 277 | Barry Hughes | 355 | Scott Puttergill | 433 | Ann Tonks |
| 278 | Jean Hughes | 356 | Paul Tunnicliffe | 434 | Ray Tonks |
| 279 | Martyn Whittall | 357 | John R Jones | 435 | Carl Hollis |
| 280 | Richard Whittall | 358 | Cliff Price | 436 | Craig Belmore |
| 281 | Danielle Whittall | 359 | Martin Price | 437 | Max Belmore |
| 282 | Mick Morris | 360 | Christopher Price | 438 | Jonathan Slim |
| 283 | R Davies | 361 | Peter Moore | 439 | John Court |
| 284 | Gary Ross | 362 | David Moore | 440 | Hannah Court |
| 285 | Gaynor Thornton | 363 | Christopher Moore | 441 | John Watts |
| 286 | Kayley Humble | 364 | James Richard Haywood | 442 | S G Moore |
| 287 | Charlie Silk | 365 | Kevin Williams | 443 | John Ross |
| 288 | Georgia Silk | 366 | Steve Harrison | 444 | Stephen John Watson |
| 289 | Thomas B Flavell | 367 | Daniel Collins | 445 | Lewis Conrad Watson |
| 290 | Richard J Weston | 368 | Rob Clutton | 446 | Stian Bøe |
| 291 | David Brown | 369 | Harvey Daly | 447 | Fred Tromans |
| 292 | Daniel Taylor | 370 | Mark Andre Ward | 448 | Søren Jensen |
| 293 | John Bates | 371 | Peter Turner | 449 | Natalie Jayne Priest |
| 294 | Philip Bates | 372 | Nicola Derrer | 450 | Daniel Nathan Woodward |
| 295 | Keith Woolridge | 373 | Baz Jones | 451 | Sarah Churm |
| 296 | Brian Vahey | 374 | Rob Jones | 452 | Adam Kenny |
| 297 | Martin Foster | 375 | John Gaughey | 453 | Tony Kenny |
| 298 | Jonathan Hillier | 376 | Colin Blount | 454 | Peter Hodges |
| 299 | Andy Saunders | 377 | Christopher Price | 455 | Ray Sears |
| 300 | Andy Partridge | 378 | Ernie Hall | 456 | Val Sears |

# ALSO AVAILABLE

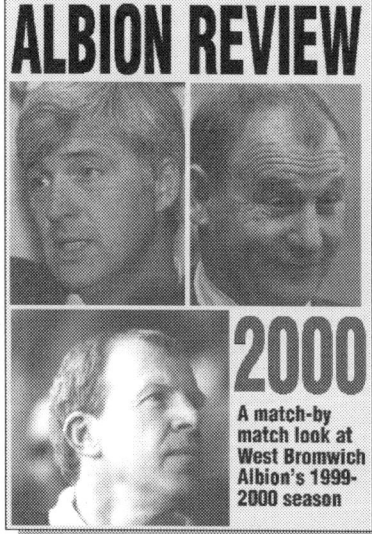

*King of The Hawthorns* and *SuperBob!* are £9.99, *Albion Reviews 2000, 2001* and *2002* are £8.85 (all prices inclusive of p&p) Please send a cheque (payable to 'The Baggies' to: The Baggies, 54 Newhall Street, West Bromwich B70 7DJ *Baggies* subscriptions are £21 annually.